THIS BOOK IS FOR YOU IF Y

- make this Lent a time of encou...

- discover Jesus, or rather Yeshua, as he was -
  a Galilean Jew and prophet;

- find out what happened in Jesus' final journey to
  Jerusalem (which no one ever tells you);

- enter into the drama of each episode of Jesus'
  eight last days;

- have a front row seat at the Last Supper;

- experience the cliff-hanging twists of the trials of
  Jesus on Good Friday;

- reflect on the crucifixion of Jesus on each day of
  Holy Week;

- read the story of Jesus' resurrection and make sense
  of the different gospel accounts;

- take up a daily practical suggestion of prayer or
  action, to make the experience of Jesus part of
  your life.

WHAT PEOPLE SAY

A LETTER FROM BISHOP ROB GILLION

Hi Andrew

Thank so much for sending me your Lent course.

I had an initial browse and then kept reading!! It is very easy to engage with. Your style is wonderfully conversational, drawing the audience into the life of 'Yeshua' and his disciples in a very imaginative and challenging way. You capture brilliantly the culture of 'Yeshua's' time followed by reflections appropriate for us today, encouraging us to live our faith.

As Bishop of the Arts especially the Performing Arts, I love your description of 'entering the drama of each episode' and 'having a front row seat at the Last Supper' and look forward to the journey with my parish this coming Lent.

I am very happy to commend 'Journey through Lent with Jesus' wholeheartedly.

Every blessing

Rob

ABOUT THE AUTHOR

Andy Roland was born of a German Jewish father and a Christian mother, so his interest in the Jewish aspects of the Christian faith came naturally. He studied history at Oxford and there became convinced of the essential reliability of the Gospel of Mark. After nine years in personnel management, he was moved on to seek ordination within the Church of England. He read theology at Durham University and was ordained in 1984. He then worked for 31 years in parishes in south London.

Since retiring in 2015 he has become engrossed in writing. His books include 'Bible in Brief', a six month exploration of the Bible, 'Discovering Psalms as Prayer', 'The Book of Job for Public Performance', 'A Week of Prayer in Jeruslaem' and a historical novel with biblical back-up, 'Jesus the Troublemaker'. He also writes monthly blogs on his website www.bibleinbrief.org.

He lives in Earls Court with his wife Linda. They are keen film-goers, going to the cinema at least once a week. He loves classical music and exploring historical places, especially the wonderful city of London.

DEDICATION

This book is dedicated to the suffering Christians
of the Middle East.

Their courage, endurance and devotion to their faith
is what makes the Holy Land holy.

Journey

THROUGH LENT
WITH JESUS

REV ANDY ROLAND

Published by Filament Publishing Ltd
16, Croydon Road, Waddon, Croydon, Surrey CR0 4PA

The right of Andrew Roland to be identified as the author of
this work has been asserted by him in accordance with
the Design and Copyright Act 1988

© Andrew Roland 2022

Printed by 4Edge

ISBN 978-1-913623-87-6

Designed by Clare Clarke
Cover by Nat Gillett
Illustrations by Daniel Gould

Cover picture based on drawing of Jerusalem
by David Roberts 1842

CONTENTS

LIST OF ILLUSTRATIONS

FOREWORD

'A passion narrative with an extended introduction' – that is how the German theologian Martin Kähler described the Gospel of Mark. That same sense of an end-loaded narrative is powerfully conveyed in Andy Roland's *Journey through Lent with Jesus*. We start out already on the road to Jerusalem, and every day takes us inexorably nearer to the climactic events of Crucifixion and Resurrection. Of all the four evangelists, it is Mark who most directly, urgently and viscerally propels us forward on the way, and this book irresistibly reflects the Marcan tempo.

But Roland and Kähler part company over how this greatest of all plots is grounded in the known or imagined reality of the human story. Kähler's famous quote was from his manifesto *'The so-called historical Jesus and the historic, biblical Christ'* (1892), where he repudiated any effort to speculate about Jesus' motivations or to reconstruct the details of his life. In these pages, by contrast, you will be invited speculatively to enter into Jesus' thinking and that of his disciples, and imaginatively to picture the scenes and society in which the Lord lived and died his last days. Andy Roland brings to this work a warm and informed knowledge of the Jewish context of His life, death and resurrection; that means that Gentile readers, at least, are constantly being reminded what an irreducibly challenging and different character Jesus was.

But the joy of this book is that, even as it establishes the strangeness of the Messianic story, it also provides lots of ways through which its unsettling and transforming power can reach deep inside us: reimagined dialogue, personal anecdote, historical explanation, spiritual guidance are all there to hook the story and its reality into our lives. The fifty daily sections take us through Lent to Good Friday and Easter, and the wealth of material for each day paces our journey even as we are irresistibly carried forward. This is a book which reimagines and retells the gospel story not simply so we can read through it but so we can work through it; and in working through it we may find that the story of our own lives is being reimagined and retold.

Dr Michael Ipgrave, Bishop of Lichfield
Chair of the Council of Christians and Jews

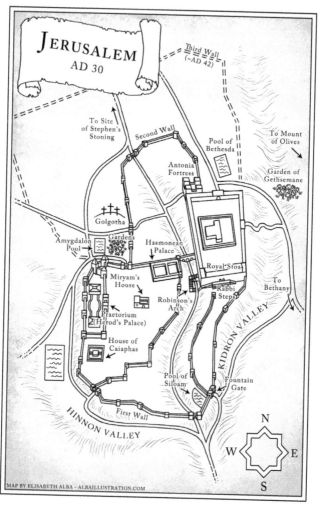

JERUSALEM
AD 30

Third Wall
(~AD 42)

To Site
of Stephen's
Stoning

Second Wall

Pool of
Bethesda

To Mount
of Olives

Antonia
Fortress

Garden of
Gethsemane

Golgotha

Gardens

Amygdalon
Pool

Hasmonean
Palace

Royal Stoa

Miryam's
House

Robinson's
Arch

Rabbi
Steps

To
Bethany

Praetorium
(Herod's Palace)

House of
Caiaphas

Pool of
Siloam

Fountain
Gate

KIDRON VALLEY

First Wall

HINNON VALLEY

N
W   E
S

MAP BY ELISABETH ALBA - ALBAILLUSTRATION.COM

© Elisabeth Alba

12

INTRODUCTION

FASCINATED BY JESUS

All my life I have been fascinated by Jesus, especially as he is portrayed in the Gospel of Mark. Since studying history at Oxford, I have been persuaded that Mark is the nearest we have to a first-hand account of Jesus. The figure of Jesus presented there is vibrant, urgent and often surprising. For instance, when he healed the leper in Mark 1.40-44, we are told, in the NRSV translation that he was 'moved with pity' and that he 'sternly warned him'. The actual Greek text says that he was angry, and that he 'snorted like a horse'. Both descriptions are omitted by Matthew and Luke. Mark shows us a Jesus who was much more striking and unsettling than our traditional pictures of him, or even of what Bible translators felt able to put before the public. Certainly Jesus was not 'meek and mild'!

This Lent book travels through the last eight days of the life of Jesus, the rabbi from Galilee, the disturber of the Temple, up to his degrading death on the cross and beyond. We follow him day by day, sometimes hour by hour, using the gospel accounts. Each one is followed by an imagined scene from my book 'Jesus the Troublemaker'.

JESUS THE TROUBLEMAKER

In September 2020 I was about to write a straightforward account of the last week of Jesus' life. To my surprise an opening sentence popped into my mind: 'It was hot in the Jordan valley'. I realised that it was going to be a historical novel! It started me on a two month journey discovering the real Jesus at the climax of his life.

I had to be quite precise about place and time and used both biblical research and imagination to create a convincing story. For instance, it takes five hours to roast a whole sheep for Passover. I also had to think through the words of Jesus so as to translate them into 21st century idioms. So when Jesus says to Simon "Satan has demanded to sift all of you like wheat" (Luke 22.31), I use the phrase, "The Enemy has insisted on putting all of you through the shredder."

Hilary Mantel, talking about her trilogy of historical novels about Thomas Cromwell, said, "Where the record fades from the page, where there is simply dot - dot - dot, I like to build on the knowledge we have, then say to myself, in the light of what we do know, what is plausible, what is possible?" That is exactly how I tried to write.

The book is available both in print, in a colour edition, as an e-book and in audio. The audio version in particular would bring the story alive in a different way.

A BOOK FOR LENT

'Journey through Lent with Jesus' has fifty daily sections reflecting on the last eight days of Jesus' life, using primarily the gospel of Mark. There are fifty sections, not forty, because the traditional forty days of Lent do not include either the six Sundays of Lent, or the four day from Maundy Thursday to Easter. This of course means that the readings are not quite in sync with the liturgical year, but they are not far off. The fourth week goes through the Last Supper in detail. Passion Week tells the story of the trials of Jesus in front of the chief priests and Pilate. In Holy Week we reflect on the crucifixion itself.

The setting of each reading is brought to life with selected passages from 'Jesus the Troublemaker'. The aim is to make the person of Jesus as vivid as possible. By concentrating on Jesus' last eight days, we can enter in greater detail into the drama of his last week, and consider parts of the story that are often left out in church. Each week starts with an illustration or a map.

Each day is made up of five elements:

1 the gospel passage;
2 the story as retold in 'Jesus the Troublemaker';
3 comments on making sense of the different accounts in the gospels and discussing issues of location and timing;
4 a short personal reflection;
5 a suggestion of something one can actually do in response.

My hope is that 'Journey through Lent with Jesus' will engage both mind and heart, and prepare us for the great turnabout of Easter.

WHAT'S IN A NAME?

Jesus was not called Jesus. Nor was Simon Peter called Simon Peter. Their language was Aramaic, not Greek. Two problems arose when Greek became the Church's language. First, Greek had no way of writing the sound 'sh'. Second, the normal Greek ending of -us, -on, -ou etc. were added. Jesus' actual name was Yeshua. Simon Peter's actual name was Shim'on Kefa (which is what St Paul used). In 'Jesus the Troublemaker' all the names are taken from the Jewish New Testament, edited by David H Stern. Quotations from the Bible use the traditional names.

A NOTE ON THE GOSPELS

As I implied at the start, my primary source is the Gospel of Mark. My guess is that it was written around 50 AD, some twenty years after the first Good Friday and Easter Day, roughly the same time as Paul wrote his main letters.

Luke's Gospel is a second-hand account. I place it about 60 AD, with Luke collecting the material for his account during the two years that Paul was in prison in Caesarea. (Luke 1.1-4, Acts 24.24-27). Later Luke inserted most of Mark in long passages into what he had already collected. It is clear, however, that he had his own sources for the Last Supper, and for Jesus' trials and execution.

My attitude to John's gospel was revolutionised by Richard Baukham's book, *'The Testimony of the Beloved Disciple'*. I now believe that it was written by a Jerusalem disciple, outside the Galilean circle of the Twelve. His Jerusalem locations are accurate, and his witness to events worth taking seriously. The long speeches and dialogues may be using classical norms, much as Plato wrote the dialogues of Socrates.

Matthew, I am sorry to say, editorialises. Where his account is not supported by the other gospels, I do not use him. However, he is a superb organiser and writes smoothly. Sadly, he is also the source of much of the Church's later anti-semitism, especially the 'blood libel', *"His blood be on us and on our children"*. (Matthew 27.25)

AND SO TO READ...

The story starts on Ash Wednesday, with quite a long journey ahead of Jesus. He is teaching his disciples about what to expect, has yet to reach Jericho and from there will have to slog up the18 mile rocky road to Jerusalem and the Temple. It was hot in the Jordan valley...

QUESTIONS FOR GROUP DISCUSSION

Although 'Journey through Lent with Jesus' is written principally for individuals to reflect on during the six weeks of Lent, it can also be used as the basis for weekly group discussions. Here are some suggested guidelines and questions to consider.

ASH WEDNESDAY AND THE NEXT THREE DAYS - THE PILGRIM ROAD
1   What would we be feeling if we were with Jesus on the pilgrim road, and heard Jesus foretell his death?
2   Does the story of Zacchaeus' surprise us?

LENT 1 - JOURNEY TO JERUSALEM
1   What did Jesus mean when he said to Bar-Timaeus, *"Your faith has healed you"?*
2   What was Jesus' attitude towards Jerusalem and the Temple?

LENT 2 - CONFRONTATION
1   What was the nature of Jesus' authority?
2   What was wrong with the Temple hierarchy?

LENT 3 - SHADOWS OF THE STORM
1   The destruction of Jerusalem must have been unthinkable to Jesus' hearers. What similar catastrophes or overthrows can we think of in the past or in the future?
2   "Christ will cone again." We proclaim this in every eucharist/communion. What does it mean for us?

LENT 4 - THE UPPER ROOM AND GETHSEMANE
1   Can Christians learn anything from Jews, particularly in celebrating the Passover?
2   Think about the different people at Gethsemane - the disciples, the soldiers, Judas and Jesus. What were their emotions?

LENT 5 - ON TRIAL

1   A monk in the Egyptian desert once said about a visitor, *"If he does not understand my silence, how will he understand my words?"* How do you interpret Jesus' silence?
2   Annas, Caiaphas, Pilate, Herod: what do you think were their motivations?

LENT 6 - CRUCIFIXION

1   How did Jesus react to pain? How do we?
2   What for you is the core message of the cross?

EASTER - THE EMPTY TOMB

1   Do you find the story of Jesus resurrection convincing or unconvincing?
2   What is the meaning of Jesus' resurrection for you?

ASH WEDNESDAY AND THE NEXT THREE DAYS

THE PILGRIM ROAD

Judaea, Samaria and Galilee at the time of Jesus

ASH WEDNESDAY – ON THE ROAD

They were on the road, going up to Jerusalem, and Jesus was walking ahead of them; they were amazed, and those who followed were afraid.

(Mark 10.32)

INTRODUCTION

Ash Wednesday is the official start of the season of Lent. The story of Jesus' temptations by the devil is usually read in churches. Both Matthew and Luke recount how Jesus was given the opportunity of turning stones into bread, jumping unscathed from the pinnacle of the Temple and acquiring world power. At the end Luke has the telling comment, *When the devil had finished every test, he departed from him until an opportune time.* (Luke 4.13)

The word 'temptation' does not give the real meaning of the Greek word *'peirasmos'*. It means test, or time of trial. It was used of the blacksmith's process of putting metal into a furnace to burn out impurities. It can refer to any situation of stress, pressure or fear. Often the expectation of suffering is more disabling than the actual suffering itself. Jesus clearly foresaw the confrontation with the Temple authorities and subsequent execution. Every step of the five day journey on foot brought the crisis nearer. How did Jesus respond?

THE SCENE

Among the pilgrims were a couple of hundred of Galileans, men and women and a few children, who were looking not merely anxious but scared. In stark contrast to the festive and expectant atmosphere of the other pilgrim groups. Slightly ahead of them were a dozen burly bearded men, their rabbi Yeshua's trainees,

23

looking bewildered as if they were not sure what was around the next corner. And ahead of them, a solitary figure, striding fast, his body tense and his face set, Yeshua from Natzeret, the prophet from the Galil.

(Note: the full name of Galilee was Galil ha Goyim, Region of the Gentiles)

COMMENT

The picture of Jesus solitary, determined, even intimidating, is striking. Often when we are scared or worried or stressed, we withdraw into ourselves. Jesus seems to have done the same. But he did that not to avoid the coming situation, but to face it head on. His absolute trust in his Father did not stop the stress. It supported his single-mindedness and determination to follow through on God's agenda, whatever the cost.

REFLECTION

How do we respond to stress? It may be a coming interview, redundancy, relationship problems, health issues. All these things have a way of eating up our inner life, so that the worry fills our heads and nothing else can penetrate. It is no good at all to say to ourselves, "I will not think like this." Sometimes even prayer simply spirals us back into our anxieties.

Is there anything that can help? Yes - the Psalms.

SUGGESTION

We do not know what Jesus used as he marched steadily along the pilgrim road. But we do know that at the final moment on the cross, Jesus turned to the Psalms to pray.

"My God, my God, why have you forsaken me?" (Psalm 22.1)

The Psalms are devotional poetry, the hymn book of ancient Israel. They were written when the kingdoms of Israel and Judah were in their prime up to the return from exile in Babylon, a period of over five hundred years. There are many psalms of praise and thanksgiving. But the largest number of psalms are in fact songs of lament, for example:

Out of the depths I cry to you, O Lord.
Lord, hear my voice!
Let your ears be attentive
o the voice of my supplications!

(Psalms 130.1)

I first realised that it was possible to pray the psalms when I visited a Catholic ashram (or Indian monastery) in Kerala in 1985. They used the Syrian Orthodox services, the oldest Christian liturgy in India. Every morning they said the same three psalms:

51.1-17	*Have mercy on me, O God.*
	(This is also the psalm set for Ash Wednesday)
63.1-8	*O God, you are my God, I seek you*
113	*Praise the Lord!*

I found that these three psalms formed an emotional ladder from confession through trust to praise. Every day I could find myself somewhere in them. By the time I had said them every day for a fortnight, I had them by heart and could pray them anywhere. Give it a try!

For a longer description of how we can use the psalms, see my book 'Discovering Psalms as Prayer', available on Amazon, Kindle or Bibleinbrief.org

THURSDAY AFTER ASH WEDNESDAY - PREMONITIONS

"*See, we are going up to Jerusalem, and the Son of Man will be handed over to the chief priests and the scribes, and they will condemn him to death; then they will hand him over to the Gentiles; they will mock him, and spit upon him, and flog him, and kill him; and after three days he will rise again.*"

(Mark 10.33-34)

THE SCENE

After walking a couple of hours, Yeshua gave the nod for people to have a rest. The twelve sat down around him, keeping an eye out for any possible hostiles they might need to defend their rabbi from.

"Listen!" said Yeshua. "we are going up to Yerushalayim, and the Son of Man will be handed over to the leading priests and the Torah-teachers, and they will condemn him to death; then they will hand him over to the Goyim; they will mock him, and spit upon him, and flog him, and kill him; and after three days he will rise again."

The group sat stunned, mouths open, hardly able to move. There was a full two minutes' silence. Then Yeshua stretched his back, got up and said, "Time to get moving." The twelve got up too and followed him, still with shocked expressions on their faces.

COMMENT

Mark gives four occasions where Jesus tells his disciples of his forthcoming suffering and death. This is the fourth and last. How reliable is this tradition? Very reliable, because it's not quite accurate. Jesus died on Friday afternoon. He was alive again on Sunday morning. That is 36 hours, not three days. Both Matthew and Luke use an expression which is repeated in the creeds: *'On the third day he rose again'.* This is possible, using the Jewish way of calculating time. Dying before sunset on Friday is one day. Friday sundown to Saturday sundown is a second day. Saturday sundown to Sunday is a third day.

The use of the expression 'after three days' is a good indication that we have here the actual words of Jesus.

REFLECTION - PREMONITIONS

When did Jesus start to have a premonition of what would happen to him? Looking at Mark's gospel, it would have been just before he asked his disciples *"Who do people say that I am?"* (Mark 8.27). This was while he was travelling the villages north of the Sea of Galilee. Six days later he went up a mountain, probably Mount Hermon in Lebanon. Then a slow journey through Galilee, then down to Judaea and across the Jordan. Then he joined the pilgrimage road towards Jerusalem. Remember, he walked everywhere. We must be looking at a period of at least several weeks if not months.

What kind of premonition was it that Jesus experienced? Premonitions are actually not that uncommon. There were several before the Aberfan disaster when a mountain of sludge buried eighteen houses and a school. The day before, a ten-year old girl, Eryl Mae Jones, had a dream: *"Mummy, you must listen. I dreamt I went to school and there was no school there. Something black had come down all over it!"*

Seeing round the corners of time is something that some people are burdened with, perhaps especially people with a strong spiritual life. It is not a blessing. Jesus must have had the coming future appear more and more clearly in his consciousness. The disciples were happily able to push it aside: *"He must be talking in parables again."* *"He's just having a bad hair day."*

The result for Jesus must have been an increase in loneliness. To be misunderstood by those closest to you is the worst kind of misunderstanding. The disciples were fixated on their dreams of the future. *"We had hoped that he was the one to redeem Israel."* (Luke 24.21). Jesus knew that that was not going to happen.

REFLECTION – THE COMING TEST

Jesus talks of a drama in six acts.

1   Jesus is to be handed over to the chief priests and scribes. The leading priests were a wealthy, powerful tight-knit and unpopular group. In 'Jesus the Troublemaker' they are called the Temple aristocrats, the scribes are Torah-teachers. Caiaphas' palace even had its own dungeon. The phrase *'will be handed over'* could signify that it was an action by God. Or that it was an inevitable part of Israel's spiritual rebellion against God's will.

2   The authorities would condemn him to death. On what grounds is unclear. Jesus certainly took actions which made them say, *"It is better for you that one man die for the people than to have the whole nation destroyed."* (John 11.50)

3   They would then hand Jesus over to the Roman military governor. (This was not part of Jesus' earlier premonitions). This is a surprise. There were other ways of dealing with opposition figures. The stoning of Stephen (Acts 7.58) and imprisonment of the church members (Acts 8.3) are examples. The Sanhedrin was the main political authority in

Judaea, though it may have had to have some of its decisions rubber stamped by the Roman Prefect. James son of Zebedee was killed by the sword on the orders of Herod Agrippa I. (Acts 12.2)

4   Jesus would be mocked, insulted and scourged. The latter could have been the Jewish flogging of 39 lashes which Paul had to suffer five times (2 Corinthians 11.24). Or it could be the vicious flogging which was a normal prelude to the Roman punishment of crucifixion.

5   Jesus would then be killed. The manner of his death is unclear.

6   After three days he would rise again. From the disciples' viewpoint, that would imply the end of the world. Resurrection was going to happen at the close of history. When Jesus says to Martha after the death of Lazarus, *"Your brother will rise again,"* she replies, *"I know he will rise again in the resurrection on the last day."* (John 11.23-24). What actually happened surprised everyone.

REFLECTION - PRAYER

Loneliness, fear, uncertainty must have been Jesus' constant companions. Yet every moment of the next eight days we see Jesus acting with precision, boldness and authority. How did he do that? The answer was his life of prayer. Specifically, his prayer as set out in the Lord's Prayer. Indeed, you could see that as not just as a prayer but as his manifesto. Virtually every line reflects Jesus' own emphasis rather than standard Jewish or rabbinical prayers. Here is the account of the prayer in Luke 11.2-5.

Father

Jesus' signature way of talking to God. Be intimate with him!

Hallowed be your name

Fundamental to all Jewish prayer. Lifting our hearts beyond ourselves.

Your kingdom come

Jesus' main message from the start, see Mark 1.15.
Love not hate is the name of the game.

Give us each day our daily bread, (or necessary bread, or tomorrow's bread)

It means radical dependence.

Forgive us our sins, as we forgive everyone indebted to us.

Our forgiving is crucial.

Do not bring us to the time of trial - even though tribulation is coming.

SUGGESTION

Today, let's pray the Lord's Prayer.

When I was living in Coventry, I got to know a canon of the cathedral (who later became a bishop). He told me that his practice of prayer was to say the Lord's Prayer once a day. But it took him an hour to pray it. I suggest we spend some significant time praying the Lord's Prayer, one petition at a time, both listening to God and talking to him. As Rabbi Lionel Blue said, *"Prayer is when God speaks to us."*

FRIDAY AFTER ASH WEDNESDAY

1. AMBITION

James and John said to Jesus, "Grant us to sit, one at your right hand and one at your left, in your glory." But Jesus said to them, "You do not know what you are asking..."

(Mark 10.37-38)

What a disappointment! Almost immediately after Jesus foretold his suffering and death, along come two brothers from his inner circle, his most trusted disciples, asking him to write them a blank cheque. "Teacher, we want you to do for us whatever we ask of you." Jesus emphasises the cost - a cup of suffering, a baptism of suffering. Here is how the scene is portayed in 'Jesus the Troublemaker':

THE SCENE

Two hours later they had another break. Two of the group, clearly brothers, asked in a low, somewhat embarrassed voice, if they could talk to him beyond the group's hearing. They moved a few yards away.

"So, what do my two thunder-lads want?"

Ya'akov, the elder, spoke. *"Rabbi, we want you to say yes to the favour we're going to ask."*

A light smile came to Yeshua's face. *"That sounds like a serious ask. What is it?"*

"When you come to reign as king, can I be your right-hand man? Can Yehoanan and I be your two chief ministers?"

31

Yeshua drew a deep breath and looked steadily from one to the other. They shifted uneasily as they tried and failed to meet his direct gaze. He said,

"You haven't a clue what you're asking. Can you pass the test I will be taking? Or can you sign up for the same struggle?"

"Yes, Rabbi, I'm sure we can!"

"Well, you will undergo the same test as I will, and you will sign up for the same struggle, but as for being my two right-hand men, I'm not in control of that. I can't make any promises."

COMMENT

This is an embarrassing story for the Early Church to circulate. Two of their leaders are shown in a pretty poor light, much like Simon Peter's denial of knowing Jesus at all on the night of his master's arrest. Indeed, Matthew changes the scene, and the one making the request is their mother, a good Jewish mother wanting to get her boys onto a good thing. (Matthew 20.20-28)

There is a parallel story earlier in Mark 9.33-37, taking place in Capernaum, in which the twelve have an angry discussion on the road as to who is the most important. Small groups can be hotbeds of jealousy and argument. Ask any member of a bowls club committee!

REFLECTION

We all have to deal with difficult people in our lives. Some are needy and vulnerable in a straightforward way. Some are like James and John, with a strong streak of manipulative egoism. That can of course include ourselves. So how does Jesus respond to his difficult disciples?

He responds with amazing tolerance! First of all, he doesn't try to second guess what they want. He simply asks them what it's about. What a lot less trouble there would be in the world if we just asked people what they're after instead of responding negatively to what we think they want. I remember being asked for money from a young homeless man just outside the National Film Theatre. I asked him what he really wanted. He replied, someone to help him mend his motorbike so he could become a delivery rider.

When James and John make their outrageous request, Jesus gives no word of criticism. First, he emphasises the cost of what they want. When they say, that's fine with us, Jesus simply withdraws himself from the equation: *"to sit at my right hand or at my left is not mine to grant."* Withdrawing like that is quite hard to do. Especially for men with a 'Mr Fix-it' mentality. But it is the root of the Christian lifestyle, summed up in the words of John the Baptist, *"He must increase but I must decrease"* (John 3.30)

SUGGESTION

A very useful prayer is the one by the American theologian Reinhold Niehbuhr and popularised around the world by Alcoholics Anonymous.

> God, grant me the serenity
> to accept the things I cannot change,
> courage to change the things I can,
> and the wisdom to know the difference.

2. JEALOUSY

When the ten heard this, they began to be angry with James and John. So Jesus called them and said to them, "Whoever wishes to become great among you must be your servant, and whoever wishes to be first among you must be slave of all."

(Mark 10.41, 43-44)

THE SCENE

What follows from the conversations between the brothers and Jesus is entirely predictable - a group explosion!

> *"I can't believe that you had the brass neck!"*
> *"What chutzpah!"*
> *"We really know who our friends are now, don't we!"*

Yeshua quickly rejoined his trainees. *"Settle down, lads, settle down. You've got it all wrong. Listen, you know that anyone who wants to climb the greasy pole in Herod's court or in Pilate's palace, they're self-important, they expect everyone to kow-tow to them and they collect people to look up at them as their patrons. It won't be like that with you. Here anyone who wants to be important must do the washing up. In my world, the way of getting to the top is to stay at the bottom. Even I didn't come to have people do things for me. I came to do things for them."*

REFLECTION

Is it right for a Christian, or anyone wanting to live a spiritual life, to be ambitious?

Jesus is clear - the answer is, no. Or is it?

The Answer is No

Jesus gives two examples of ambition. The first is to be seen and known as the top dog. To have the biggest office, the thickest carpet, the most expensive company car. The other is to call the shots. *"When I say jump, you jump." "The buck stops here."*

There are several downsides to this way of living. The first is stress - the stress of constant decision-making. Six months after Nick Clegg became part of a Conservative - Lib Dem coalition, he was asked what it was like being Deputy Prime Minister. He replied, *"It's like being slowly lobotomised."*

The second is lack of information. The more layers there between you and the actual effect of your decisions in the real world, the less you know what is actually going on. There was a recent television series in which bosses went undercover in their own organisations. I saw the one where the Managing Director of Pickfords spent a month as a new employee on several removal vans. He was shocked! At how little he paid his staff, the conditions that some of them worked in, their need to sleep in their vans on overnight jobs. At the end he raised all their wages, apologised to the staff at the sub-standard depot in south-east London, and paid for driving lessons for one young man. How did he learn about all this? By becoming a servant.

The third is your popularity is bought. There are plenty of cases where wealthy people lose all their friends when they fall from grace. The classic tale is 'Timon of Athens' by Shakespeare.

Being a servant is what connects us to the real world. It is charities who show us what life is really like among the trouble spots of the world, not government ministers. It is absolutely what the Church (including vicars and bishops) is called to.

The Answer is Yes

Jesus was ambitious.

"I came to bring fire to the earth, and how I wish it were already kindled!"

(Luke 12.49)

Jesus was ambitious for his call from God. All of us have the potential to be the best artist or technician, blogger or carer, man or woman that we can be. Whatever we do with passion is our calling and it is right for us to be ambitious to do it as well as possible. There is just one caveat or warning.

Put away from you all bitterness and wrath and anger and wrangling and slander, together with all malice, and be kind to one another, tender-hearted, forgiving one another, as God in Christ has forgiven you.

(Ephesians 4.31-32)

No jealousy or envy. The litmus test is whether or not we are pleased if someone does something better than us! But let's not be too hard on ourselves. We are all works-in-progress.

SUGGESTION

Here are two simple and useful prayers:

For myself:
Father, thank you for my gifts. Please amend my faults.

And for other people:
Father, thank you for their gifts. Please amend their faults.

Good luck!

SATURDAY AFTER ASH WEDNESDAY – A CHANGE OF HEART

Jesus looked up and said, 'Zacchaeus, hurry and come down; for I must stay at your house today.' So he hurried down and was happy to welcome him. All who saw it began to grumble and said, 'He has gone to be the guest of one who is a sinner.'

(Luke19.1-7)

This is perhaps my favourite story about Jesus, because I think it gives a real insight into Jesus' inner life. It is also a story which is misrepresented in most people's minds. Zacchaeus' repentance did not come before Jesus invited himself, it came after. And Jesus did not invite himself for a meal. He invited himself for the whole weekend! Here is how I imagine the scene played out in 'Jesus the Troublemaker':

THE SCENE

As they made their way between the square whitewashed houses and their security walls, the street filled with yet more villagers. Then, in the distance, almost where the large two-storey stone villas could be seen, Yeshua stopped and looked curiously at a tree two hundred paces away.

He leant towards an elderly man near him and asked,

"Who's the man up that tree?"

The man looked up and his mouth dropped open in surprise. With a grimace he said,

"I can't believe it. That's - that's Zakkai! What's he doing in our part of town? And up a tree, in the name of Aalah!"

37

"And just who is Zakkai?"

"Only the head of the tax farmers in the region. And, by Aalah, doesn't he farm the taxes well. He's a swindler, an extortioner, a miser and a Roman toady. He's got half our town in debt to pay for his rake-off. His name Zakkai - Righteous - what a joke! And now, unbelievably, he's climbing a tree! Doesn't he have any dignity?"

"I can see why he's unpopular," said Yeshua thoughtfully. *"But still,"* he smiled disconcertingly, *"he does climb trees."*

A couple of minutes later they reached the spot where Zakkai, in an incongruously ornate cloak, was clinging to a branch, trying to look as if he wasn't there. A few of the braver elements of the crowd spat in his direction.

Yeshua stopped and called out,

"Zakkai!"

The little man almost fell off the branch with shock.

"Zakkai, you'd better shin down. I'm staying at your place this weekend!"

The adoring crowd quickly changed their tune.

"Unbelievable!" *"Is he a real prophet?"* *"You can't trust Galileans."* *"What a fake!".*

Yeshua just stood there amid the turmoil, waiting while Zakkai tumbled down the tree. He stood in front of Yeshua, twigs and leaf dust in his hair and on his torn robe. Open-mouthed, trying to gather his wits.

"R-rabbi - you're coming to my house? Really?"

"If you'll have me."

"Rabbi - I don't know what to say. I've not lived well." He gathered his wits. *"Listen, tell you what I'll do. I'm going to give half of my possessions to people on the breadline. And if I've cheated anyone - "* the crowd murmured, *'Who haven't you?'* - *"anyway, I'll pay them back not double but four times over!"*

The crowd stood in stunned silence for a moment, then shouts erupted, *"Good ol' Zak !"* *"Blessings on you, Zakkai!"* *"Three cheers for Zak!"*

Yeshua looked round grinning, then shouted, *"Today - today - salvation has come to this man! This son of Abraham. This fellow Jew! This righteous man! Come on, Zakkai, lead the way."*

The whole delighted crowd followed Yeshua and Zakkai out of the village to a large ornate villa, none happier than Yeshua's twelve trainees, looking forward to their first comfortable night's sleep for five days.

COMMENT

Even though Luke is a secondary source, and no other gospel mentions Zacchaeus, I know of no other story of Jesus which so clearly describes his reactions to people. The key is not to say "Well, Jesus was God, so he knew everything, so he knew all about Zacchaeus and that he was ready to repent etc." By concentrating on his divinity you effectively reject his humanity. It's as a very human person that he is an inspiration for our lives today.

REFLECTION

The key to this story is that in the Middle East, adults of any kind of dignity did not climb trees. It is something children do. There is a story of the British ambassador in Egypt during the time of Nasser, the 1960s. Playing in the garden with his children, a ball got caught in a tree, and the ambassador climbed up to get it. A couple of weeks later he had a regular meeting with Nasser, which got off to quite an awkward start. Eventually Nasser leaned forwards and asked, *"Mr Ambassador, is it true you climbed a tree in your garden?"* It was an unbelievable story for him. He was quite unbothered that he was revealing that the gardeners were security spies.

The whole story in Luke shows that Jesus had retained his childlikeness, that he had not 'learnt the dirty devices of this world'. (Traherne, Centuries). He was able to see the world afresh without judgement. All he noted about Zacchaeus was that, despite his corrupt dealings, he had retained an element of the child within. Jesus responded directly to that. For Zacchaeaus, Jesus' acceptance of him was transformative.

SUGGESTION

Here are two passages to read to awaken our sense of wonder and praise:

'You never enjoy the world aright, till the Sea itself floweth in your veins, till you are clothed with the heavens, and crowned with the stars: and perceive yourself to be the sole heir of the whole world, and more than so, because men are in it who are every one sole

heirs as well as you. Till you can sing and rejoice and delight in
God, as misers do in gold, and Kings in sceptres, you never enjoy
the world.'

(Thomas Traherne (1636 - 1674),
Centuries of Meditation)

Teach me, my God and King,
     In all things Thee to see,
And what I do in anything
     To do it as for Thee.

A man that looks on glass,
     On it may stay his eye;
Or if he pleaseth, through it pass,
     And then the heav'n espy.

All may of Thee partake:
     Nothing can be so mean,
Which with his tincture—"for Thy sake"—
     Will not grow bright and clean.

A servant with this clause
     Makes drudgery divine:
Who sweeps a room as for Thy laws,
     Makes that and th' action fine.

This is the famous stone
     That turneth all to gold;
For that which God doth touch and own
     Cannot for less be told.

('The Elixir' by George Herbert, 1633
amended by John Wesley 1738)

LENT 1

JOURNEY TO JERUSALEM

The Temple

SUNDAY OF LENT 1 – BAR-TIMAEUS

*A*s Jesus and his disciples and a large crowd were leaving
Jericho, Bartimaeus son of Timaeus, a blind beggar, was
*sitting by the roadside. When he heard that it was Jesus of
Nazareth, he began to shout out and say, 'Jesus, Son of David,
have mercy on me!' Many sternly ordered him to be quiet, but he
cried out even more loudly, 'Son of David, have mercy on me!'
Jesus stood still and said, 'Call him here.' … So throwing off his
cloak, he sprang up and came to Jesus. Then Jesus said to him,
'What do you want me to do for you?' The blind man said to
him, 'My teacher, let me see again.' Jesus said to him, 'Go; your
faith has made you well.' Immediately he regained his sight and
followed him on the way.*

(Mark 10.46-52)

INTRODUCTION

If the traditional dating of Palm Sunday is correct, then
Jesus stayed two days in Zacchaeus' house, keeping the
sabbath and speaking at the synagogue. (However, if John
is right about the anointing at Bethany, then this would be a
Thursday, see John 12.1).

Whatever day it was, Jesus and his disciples started off early,
at first light, 6.00 am. They had an eighteen mile trek ahead
of them. Bar-Timaeus (son of Timai) was also up early to
start begging before the sun got too hot.

Here is how I imagined the scene:

THE SCENE

> *"Brothers, what's all this crowd? You're not all going up to
> Yerushalayim, surely?"*

45

"Brother, it's a great day for us. We're seeing off the prophet Yeshua from Natzeret. He stayed with us all weekend - at the house of Zakkai, would you believe!"

The blind beggar shouted out, *"Yeshua, Ben-David, take pity on me!"*

"Bar-Timai, what are you thinking of, using the Hebrew royal title like that. You'll get us all into trouble."

"Yeshua, Ben-David, take pity on me!!"

"That's enough, Bar-Timai, stop your noise, enough already!"

"BEN-DAVID, TAKE PITY ON ME!!!"

Yeshua had walked on several yards since the beggar had started asking about him. He now stopped, and said, *"Tell him to come here."*

"Courage, brother, get up, he's asking for you."

The blind beggar jumped up, tossing aside his cloak, and ran stumbling in the direction of where he thought Yeshua was standing, helped by members of the crowd. Yeshua grasped the man's shoulders, so he was standing upright facing him.

"So - what do you want me to do for you?"

"Rabbani, let me see again!"

Yeshua paused, his hands still on the beggar's shoulders. Then he announced,

"Your trust has already healed you."

Then Yeshua kissed him on both cheeks.

The man stood stock still. He blinked several times, rubbed his eyes with the back of his hands, then cried out, *"I CAN SEE! PRAISE GOD! Rabbani, can I come with you?"*

Yeshua's face broke into a broad smile. *"Certainly. Come along."* Yeshua strode smartly up the steep rocky road that led towards the Temple. Bar-Timai ran back to collect his cloak - he would need it in the chilly Yerushalayim night air - and followed Yeshua on the way.

COMMENT

Both Mark and Luke tell the story of the healing of Bar-Timaeus. (We don't know what his first name was). Matthew bizarrely has two blind men being healed (Matthew 20.29-34), perhaps to indicate that this was a regular activity for Jesus.

Mark and Luke are identical, except that Luke places it at Jesus' entry into Jericho (Luke 18.35-43) while Mark places it at his departure. I believe Mark is correct. Luke added Mark to his material secondarily, and the Bar-Timaeus story comes at the end of a longer continuous passage from Mark (Luke 18.15-43).

When we are told that Bar-Timaeus 'followed Yeshua on the way', it could simply mean the physical road leading to Jerusalem. The Way was also the first name given to the followers of Jesus after the resurrection (Acts 9.2).

REFLECTION

How was Bar-Timaeus healed?

Jesus did not say *"I heal you."*
He did not pray, *"Please, Father, heal this man."*
He did not say *"God has healed you."*
He DID say, *"Your faith/your trust has healed you."*
And he did not say, *"It's because of your lack of faith you were not healed before."*

So what was happening?
Was Jesus lying? (Actually I did heal him).
Was he half-lying? (I did have something to do with it, but Bar-Timaeus helped)
Was he telling the truth? (It really was Bar-Timaeus' faith which did the healing).

One way of looking at it is that Jesus, because of his relationship with his Father, was the natural bearer of God's life and love. It was the beggar's desperation and persistence which drove him to come inside the circle of the the Spirit's power which resided in Jesus.

In an earlier instance, Jesus was walking through a dense crowd, when an elderly woman with internal bleeding reached out and touched his cloak.

The woman came up behind Jesus in the crowd and touched his cloak, for she said, 'If I but touch his clothes, I will be made well.' Immediately her haemorrhage stopped; and she felt in her body that she was healed of her disease.

Immediately aware that power had gone forth from him, Jesus turned about in the crowd and said, 'Who touched my clothes?'... The woman, knowing what had happened to her, came in fear and trembling, fell down before him, and told him the whole truth. He said to her, 'Daughter, your faith has made you well; go in peace, and be healed of your disease.'

(Mark 5.27-34, ed.)

What do you think?

SUGGESTION

How can we step into the active presence of God's life and love? One way is to practise Ignatian meditation.

Ignatian meditation was devised by Ignatius Loyola (1491 - 1556) when he founded the Society of Jesus. He conceived of it as a missionary community of 'contemplatives in action'. When he was about thirty, he wrote 'Spiritual Exercises', a month of meditation exercises to help people discern the will of God. It was finally published in English in 1951 and is now used in all Christian traditions, particularly in the form of the 'nineteenth annotation' which describes how to use the meditation programme in the course of daily life.

The practice is described by Ignatius:

Place yourself in a scene from the Gospels. Ask yourself, *"What do I see? What do I hear? What do I feel, taste and smell?"* Having placed ourselves in the story, as one of the people there, we then see what Jesus himself may say to us. The purpose of these Exercises is that we might gain the empathy to *"follow and imitate more closely our Lord."*

Sit comfortably and take as long as you want

The story of Bar-Timaeus is an ideal one to start with. Think what it was like to be in Jericho at 6 o'clock on a spring morning 1,000 feet below sea level, at the start of the rocky road leading to Jerusalem. Imagine the people there, disciples, pilgrims, townspeople, beggars and Jesus. Where do you see yourself, where are you standing? What do you see happen? How do you react? Finally, how does Jesus address you? How do you respond?

I hope that this is a useful method to help us 'follow Jesus on the way.'

MONDAY OF LENT 1 – REGIME CHANGE

Jesus went on to tell a parable, because he was near Jerusalem, and because they supposed that the kingdom of God was to appear immediately. So he said, 'A nobleman went to a distant country to get royal power for himself and then return. He summoned ten of his slaves, and gave them ten pounds, and said to them, "Do business with these until I come back." But the citizens of his country hated him and sent a delegation after him, saying, "We do not want this man to rule over us." When he returned, having received royal power, he ordered these slaves, to whom he had given the money, to be summoned so that he might find out what they had gained by trading. The first came forward and said, "Lord, your pound has made ten more pounds." He said to him, "Well done, good slave! Because you have been trustworthy in a very small thing, take charge of ten cities." Then the second came, saying, "Lord, your pound has made five pounds." He said to him, "And you, rule over five cities." Then the other came, saying, "Lord, here is your pound. I wrapped it up in a piece of cloth, for I was afraid of you, because you are a harsh man; you take what you did not deposit, and reap what you did not sow." He said to him, "I will judge you by your own words, you wicked slave! You knew, did you, that I was a harsh man, taking what I did not deposit and reaping what I did not sow? Why then did you not put my money into the bank? Then when I returned, I could have collected it with interest." He said to the bystanders, "Take the pound from him and give it to the one who has ten pounds." (And they said to him, "Lord, he has ten pounds!") "I tell you, to all those who have, more will be given; but from those who have nothing, even what they have will be taken away. But as for these enemies of mine who did not want me to be king over them—bring them here and slaughter them in my presence." '

(Luke 19.11-27)

51

THE SCENE

Luke places this disturbing story during Jesus' final journey up to Jerusalem. Here is how I describe the setting:

The road was partially paved during the steep ascent from Yericho past Herod's castle. It flattened a bit where it joined Wadi Qelt. Here Yeshua and his followers refilled their water bottles, for there would be no more water for the next fourteen miles. The path was sometimes paved and sometimes bare limestone rock. It was hot, dry and dusty work. An hour later they passed the Roman garrison guarding the pass of Adummim, a favourite spot for bandit attacks. They had now walked for almost three hours, uphill all the way. The angle of ascent would be easier for the next six hours, and Yeshua and his followers sat for a rest among the shrubs which gave some relief from the glare of the sun on the rocky surface.

"It's a tough journey. But it'll be worth it when we see Israel saved!" said one of the followers.

"Yes, brother, the day of liberation!" exclaimed his friend.

Yeshua sighed heavily, and the group grew quiet as they waited for him to speak.

"Boys and girls, you're looking forward to a real regime change, yes?"

"Yes. Amen. Truly" were the murmured responses.

"Let me tell you about one..."

COMMENT

1 Comparison with Matthew

The story has an obvious parallel in the Parable of the Talents in Matthew 25.14-30. The difference is not just the bloodthirsty ending in Luke, nor the tidier story in Matthew with its three individual servants. The real difference is that the story in Luke is a historical event, almost unique among in Jesus' teachings. (Another reference to actual events is to Pilate's massacre of the Galilean pilgrims in 13.1-5, with a similar message of warning). In my reading of the accounts, Matthew's parable has been air-brushed to give a practical message about discipleship for the church of his time. Luke's story is of Jesus warning his followers of the impending crisis.

2 The story

Herod I, (also called Herod the Great by those who thought his rebuilding the Temple made up for all his other tyrannical acts), died about 4 B.C. Two or three years before, Herod had executed three of his sons, and bequeathed his kingdom to his younger son Antipas. Then a few days before his death he changed his will bequeathing the southern part of his kingdom - Judaea, Samaria and Idumaea - to his elder son Archelaus. Archelaus attempted to curry favour with the crowd in the Temple but ended up massacring 3,000 of them.

It is at that point that Archelaus made the two-week journey to Rome to ask Augustus Caesar to confirm the latest will. Unsurprisingly, there was a counter-delegation of fifty Jews, saying, *"We do not want this man to rule over us."* Augustus decided in favour of Herod's last will, and Archelaus made the return trip. This meant there was a month's hiatus, at least, in which there was no government in Judaea and Samaria.

It is this situation that the story is about. Archelaus gives several of his servants a 'mina' - worth about £100. Some of them make a significant profit. One of them hides it in the ground. The reason for his condemnation was that the other servants by their action had proved themselves to be Archelaus' supporters. If he had failed to be appointed ruler, they would have been marked men. The one who had hidden the money was keeping his options open, blowing with the wind, not someone to be relied on.

When Archelaus returned successful, he dismissed the high priest and executed his opponents.

3 The moral
It may be that Jesus is pointing out the drastic consequences of not being on God's side when the kingdom comes. He is calling us to nail our colours to the mast of God's future rather than to the shifting sands of human calculation. Similar perhaps to what the prophet Amos said seven hundred years before:

Alas for you who desire the day of the Lord!
Why do you want the day of the Lord?
It is darkness, not light;
as if someone fled from a lion,
and was met by a bear;
or went into the house and rested a hand against the wall,
and was bitten by a snake.
Is not the day of the Lord darkness, not light,
and gloom with no brightness in it?

(Amos 5.18-20)

REFLECTION

It is an unpleasant story. But it does speak to our condition today. With the devastation being caused by global warming, and the rise of tyrannical regimes of various colours around the world, the question does arise whether this is a world we want to bring children into.

Jesus accepts unflinchingly the power of evil and suffering in the world. Jesus' fundamental belief seems to be that where someone offers God radical obedience, God will break in to the situation.

Jesus is looking for men and women who will stand up and be counted. The challenge often takes us by surprise.

There was one occasion in the 1970s as a Personnel Officer at Imperial College when I did find the courage to do the right thing. Imperial College has a sports complex, and the manager had asked me several times to sack a part-time cleaning lady, for no discernible reason. One day I was called into the office of the Registrar, Peter Mee, quite a dominant personality and the Sports Centre manager was there. Peter Mee started off. *"Well, Mr Roland, is there any reason why we should not dismiss Mrs So-and-so?"* I did some rapid thinking. I could not think of any. She was not a union member and her hours were too few to be covered by the unfair dismissal legislation. So I said, in a rather small voice, *"It wouldn't be moral."* To my astonishment Peter Mee immediately went on to the next business.

SUGGESTION

Remember an occasion when you have stood up for what was right, however small. And thank God for that.

TUESDAY OF LENT 1 - ARRIVAL & LAMENT

When they were approaching Jerusalem, at Bethphage and Bethany, Jesus sent two of his disciples and said to them, "Go into the village ahead of you, and immediately as you enter it, you will find tied there a colt that has never been ridden; untie it and bring it."

Then they brought the colt to Jesus and threw their cloaks on it; and he sat on it. Many people spread their cloaks on the road, and others spread leafy branches that they had cut in the fields. Then those who went ahead and those who followed were shouting, "Hosanna! Blessed is the one who comes in the name of the Lord!"

As he came near and saw the city, he wept over it.

Then he entered Jerusalem and went into the temple; and when he had looked around at everything, as it was already late, he went out to Bethany with the twelve.

(Mark 11.1-2, 8-9, Luke 19.41, Mark 11.11)

THE SCENE

The next three hours of Jesus' life were full of conflicting emotions.

The story starts with Jesus and his companions having a well-earned rest, after walking for nine hours. Jesus sends two of his followers to collect a mount from the next village with the coded message *'The Lord needs it and will send it back here immediately.'* They bring back a young horse (not a donkey, see comment below). It hasn't been broken in, but Jesus calms it and rides towards Jerusalem.

It is now three o'clock in the afternoon, and many of the pilgrims who had come for Passover would be in the

Temple. But all those who had accompanied Jesus on the road enthusiastically cheered their prophet as they approached the holy city. Here is how I described it in 'Jesus the Troublemaker':

The whole group, over a hundred men and women, started praising God and crying out, *"HOSANNA! BLESSED IS HE WHO COMES IN ADONAI'S NAME! HOSANNA!"* Some cut down branches and waved them. Others put their cloaks on the path in front of Yeshua's horse. The procession made its way over the shoulder of the Mount of Olives. Where the path turned left, Yeshua stopped. Yeshua gazed at the city spread out before him, the magnificent towers, the tiled roofs, the ostentatious facade of the Temple silhouetted against the late afternoon sun, and dominating the whole city, the enormous Roman fortress of the Antonia. Silent tears started to run down Yeshua's cheeks into his beard. Suddenly, he raised his voice, keening a lament:

"Yerushlayim, Yerushalyim!
You kill the prophets!
You stone the ones sent to you!
How often I've wanted to gather your children,
as a hen gathers her chicks,
and you would not.
If only you'd known today
what makes for your shalom,*
but it's hidden from your eyes.
The days are coming upon you
when your enemies will encircle you,
dash you to the ground,
you and your children within you,
and leave not a single stone
on a stone standing

all because you did not recognise
the hour you'll be held to account."

* 'shalom' means not just peace, but prosperity, well-being, wholeness

After another moment silently taking in sight of the city, Yeshua set off down the hill, with his followers behind him. On either side of the path were hundreds of booths, temporary shelters put up by pilgrims, but with few people around. Most were still in the Temple. As the party reached the river Kidron, they started meeting pilgrims leaving the Temple. As soon as they were told that the prophet Yeshua from the Galil was making a grand entrance, excitement swelled. As more pilgrims joined in, the ones from the Galil shouting particularly loudly and exuberantly.

"PRAISE GOD! PRAISE ADONAI* THE KING OF ISRAEL! BLESSED IS HE WHO COMES IN THE NAME OF ADONAI! BLESSED IS THE COMING KINGDOM OF OUR FATHER DAVID!"

Some of them took off their cloaks and spread them on the path, so that the way leading to the Eastern Gate was like a royal carpet.

* 'Adonai' means 'Lord', and refers back to the name that God revealed to Moses at the burning bush.

When they got to the Gate, Yeshua dismounted. He strode past the Temple guards into the Temple itself.

It would not be long before the gates were closed for the night. Shadows were already lengthening. Jesus walked around the vast space of the Outer Court like any ordinary tourist, taking in the activity of the merchants who were now closing down their money-changing services; the sheep and cattle dealers, starting to drive their animals back to their pens outside the North Gate; the labourers sweeping up the dung-covered straw from the marble pavement. As he approached the centre of the Temple complex, the Court of Israel in front of the Court of the Priests, the smell of burning flesh, smoke, incense and fresh blood formed a rather sickly smell. Yeshua took it all in, but not one word or expression of his face indicated what he thought.

As the first oil lamps were lit, Yeshua said, *"Time to go, boys."* He led them outside the city, and together with the colt, made the hour's walk back to Beit-Anyah.

COMMENT

Several comments are needed to explain the story as related above:

1 Horse or donkey?
The traditional picture of Jesus' triumphal entry is that he came to the Temple riding on a donkey. It is the subject of countless sermons emphasising the humility of Jesus. It is so recorded in Matthew and John. It is the basis of a great little poem by G K Chesterton:

Fools! For I also had my hour;
One far fierce hour and sweet:
There was a shout about my ears,
And palms before my feet.

However, I think that it the traditional imagery is wrong. The word used by both Mark and Luke (following `Mark) is 'Polos'. Meaning foal or colt. Normally a horse's foal but

59

not necessarily. However, only horses need to be broken in, not donkeys, and Mark records that no one had ridden it yet. The allusion to a donkey comes in Matthew's and John's account, and both refer to the prophecy of Zechariah 9.9:

Lo, your king comes to you;
triumphant and victorious is he,
humble and riding on a donkey,
on a colt, the foal of a donkey.

2 The Secret Sign

Jesus has clearly pre-arranged the picking up of the colt beforehand through a network of secret sympathisers in the Jerusalem area. These people were not known to his Galilean followers, nor to the twelve. We have the same precautions used when Jesus arranged the venue for the Last Supper. We have already seen how prone to jealousy Jesus' closest companions were. How did they react to being kept out of the loop like this? How did Judas Iscariot react?

3 The Crowd

How big was the crowd that accompanied Jesus to the Temple? Arriving in the middle of the afternoon was going to miss out on a number of possible supporters. My guess is that the the crowd numbered in in hundreds, not thousands. It was as much a statement to the Temple authorities as a celebration for his followers.

4 Lament

Luke is the only gospel writer who mentions Jesus' lament over Jerusalem. It certainly fits the emotional nature of Jesus coming over the brow of the Mount of Olives and seeing the city laid out before him. I have included six lines from an earlier lament recorded in Luke 13.34, simply because of its incomparable poetry. I guess that Jesus intoned it as a song of lament, like so many of the psalms.

5 Reconnaissance

Jesus' entry to the Temple is frankly an anti-climax. What was he doing? He was doing what every good general or entrepreneur does, he was making a reconnaissance, just as governor Nehemiah did over four hundred years before:

"I got up during the night, I and a few men with me; I told no one what my God had put into my heart to do for Jerusalem. The only animal I took was the animal I rode. I went out by night by the Valley Gate past the Dragon's Spring and to the Dung Gate, and I inspected the walls of Jerusalem that had been broken down and its gates that had been destroyed by fire.... The officials did not know where I had gone or what I was doing; I had not yet told the Jews, the priests, the nobles, the officials, and the rest that were to do the work."

(Nehemiah 2.12-13, 16)

REFLECTION

The main impression of these few hours of Jesus' life is the multitude of contradictory emotions.

There was relief at finishing a hard day's walk.

There may have been anxiety over the arrangements for the colt.

There may have been jealousy of some of the disciple at being kept in the dark.

There was simple euphoria of the crowd of his followers and supporters as he made a public demonstration of his implicit claims to be God's ambassador to Israel.

There was grief felt by Jesus over the inevitable fate of Jerusalem.

And there was his grim resolve to take action following his scrutiny of the Temple.

The most striking of the emotions is Jesus' grief over Jerusalem. This raises the question:

Does God feel grief?

I once had a telling experience of spiritual grief. It was over forty years ago, when the charismatic movement was creating deep divisions within the evangelical part of the church. I was on a weekend break in Salisbury at a time where there was a public meeting between the respective leaders, John Stott and Michael Harper. I had started praying in the evening in my B&B room, thanking God for this meeting between John and Michael. I was suddenly overwhelmed with sobbing over the division between these faithful Christians, and this continued for half an hour. I know it was not my sorrow. I can only assume that it was God's sorrow.

SUGGESTION

The Psalms are full of lament. Let us take a situation which grieves us, and write a psalm to express our feelings, perhaps using some words of psalms like 5, 10, 12, 22, 44, 69, 81, etc.etc.

WEDNESDAY OF LENT 1 - A FEAST WITH FRIENDS

Six days before the Passover Jesus came to Bethany, the home of Lazarus, whom he had raised from the dead. There they gave a dinner for him... Mary took a pound of costly perfume made of pure nard, anointed Jesus' feet, and wiped them with her hair... Judas Iscariot said, 'Why was this perfume not sold for three hundred denarii and the money given to the poor?' Jesus said, 'Leave her alone. She bought it so that she might keep it for the day of my burial. You always have the poor with you, but you do not always have me.'

(John 12.1-8, ed.)

THE SCENE

Shim'on's house was built around a large courtyard with the main gate opening on the street. Shim'on met Yeshua and the twelve and kissed each on both cheeks, beard to beard. After two servants had washed the feet of the guests, they put their packs down in the large room where the women were going to eat, then went to stand round the brazier burning in the courtyard. Eleazar entered along with his sisters, and the men settled down to recline around the three sides of the tables. Shim'on asked Yeshua to give the blessing. He took a small loaf, broke it in half and said,

"Baruch atah Adonai Eloheinu Melech ha'olam, ha'motzi lechem min ha'aretz" - Blessed are you, Lord our God, King of the universe, who provides bread from the land. He went on to invoke the blessing on the wine. The servants came in and out, refilling the plates of lentils, vegetables and baked fish, supervised by Marta who could not bear for things not to be done properly.

Suddenly, the conversation died down. Young Miryam was standing in the doorway of the guest chamber, tears tricking down her cheeks. She entered hesitantly and knelt where Yeshua was reclining.

"Rabbi," she whispered, *"it's thanks to you that our brother is alive."* She started to weep again, choking on her tears. The tears started dripping on to Yeshua's out-stretched feet. She took a deep breath, reached up, unpinned her hair and used her long dark hair to wipe away the drops. The trainees and Eleazar shifted uncomfortably on their cushions. Yeshua acted as if nothing out of the ordinary was happening. Miryam reached into a small embroidered cloth bag tied to her belt. From it she took a delicate white translucent alabaster jar, sealed with wax. With a snap she broke off the neck of the jar and poured the most wonderful scented oil of nard* on to Yeshua's feet, smoothing it gently into the skin with her hands. She bowed down and planted a single kiss on his foot. Then rapidly she got up and went back towards the guest room. Until a man's comment froze her in her tracks.

"Rabbi, that's not right! That's a waste! You tell us always to remember the poor. That nard could have fed thirty people for a month!"

"Let her be, Y'hudah. Why do you trouble her? She's done a beautiful thing for me. You'll always have the poor with you, and you can do good for them whenever you wish. But you won't always have me. She has done what she could. She has given me my burial anointing in advance."

A shocked murmur ran round the table. Shim'on Kepha hesitantly said, *"Rabbi, I don't think we understand."*

"No, Shim'on? But you will. Indeed wherever you proclaim the message of Aalah's kingly rule** in the whole world, you will tell the story of her gift in memory of her."

Miryam stood transfixed in the doorway as she and her rabbi gazed at each other. Then, with her knees shaking she turned and stumbled back into the guest room where she collapsed in tears.

* Nard is an aromatic oil form the spikenard plant, which grows in the Himalayas.
** The kingdom of God, using the Aramaic word for God.

COMMENT

There is a problem about this story. John places it six days before Passover, presumably in the house of Lazarus, with his sister Mary weeping over Jesus. Mark 14.3-9 makes it two days before Passover, in the house of Simon the Leper, and with an unnamed woman. Luke tells of a similar event earlier in Jesus' ministry with an immoral woman at the house of Simon the Pharisee (Luke 7.36-50). I have not made use of Luke's account.

I chose to take John's account as the primary one. His traditions about Jerusalem are often accurate. Having the feast six days before Passover would make Jesus' arrival come at the start of the week's preparation for the festival, which is likely, and it would be natural way of welcoming him. In my book I compromised and made the feast four days before Passover. I think that six days is probably right, and that Jesus arrived at the Temple on Palm Thursday. But I bowed to tradition by having Jesus arrive on Sunday.

John implies that the feast was at the house of Lazarus, Mark says it was at the house of Simon the Leper, both in Bethany.

It is easy to imagine that a major act of hospitality for over twenty guests - the Twelve plus half a dozen women - might need the resources of more than one household. Perhaps Mark does not mention Lazarus and his sisters because they were the most at risk of arrest by the Temple authorities?

The reaction of some to Mary's extravagant gesture was decidedly negative. In Mark it is several disciples who criticise her, in John it is Judas Iscariot. Mark links this incident directly to Judas turning traitor. Maybe Judas felt this was another instance of Jesus treating his Jerusalem supporters with favouritism.

REFLECTION

To whom in this story do we relate to most? Mary, Judas or Jesus?

Mary
How passionate do we allow ourselves to be?
How generous are we?
How open with our emotions?

Judas
Do we tend to judge other people who do not react the way we do?
How do we balance the need to celebrate as against the need to care for those in need?
What do we feel if we think we are being left out of the loop?

Jesus

How accepting are we of other people and the way they express themselves?

How easy are we with physical affection?

When there is disagreement around us, do we seek compromise or do we fully support the most vulnerable?

SUGGESTION

Listen to Sidney Carter's song 'Judas and Mary' on YouTube.

Pray for one other person whom we get on with or with whom we don't.

"Lord, bless them and give them what they need."

THURSDAY OF LENT 1 - THE FIG TREE

On the following day, when they came from Bethany, he was hungry. Seeing in the distance a fig tree in leaf, he went to see whether perhaps he would find anything on it. When he came to it, he found nothing but leaves, for it was not the season for figs. He said to it, "May no one ever eat fruit from you again." And his disciples heard it.

(Mark 11.12-14)

THE SCENE

They reached the neighbouring village of Beit-Pagey. As they left the village behind them, Yeshua mused, *"Hmm. Beit-Pagey - 'House of Unripe Figs'. I wonder if it's true. Maybe we should try it out. I could do with some figs to finish off breakfast."*

He made for a large old fig tree standing untidily on its own on the edge of the hill. He started pushing aside the large leaves, squeezing the hard unripe buds.

"What's he doing?" muttered T'oma to Ya'akov Ben-Chalfai. *"He must know we won't get any figs for a couple of months."* *"Search me,"* responded Ya'akov.

Yeshua stood back from the tree with an almost comical look of anger on his face. He stretched out his arm, pointing directly at the fig tree and proclaimed, *"You useless fig tree! All leaves and no fruit! In the name of Adonai the King of the universe, you are cursed to be fruitless from now and for ever."* He strode off downhill, calling over his shoulder, *"Come on, lads, let's leave this house of unripe figs behind us."*

COMMENT

What a strange story. Why had Jesus got it in for fig trees?

It is the clearest example we have of Jesus performing a prophetic action, which the Old Testament prophets did regularly. Here is an example from the prophet Jeremiah, c. 598 BCE. Jerusalem is being besieged by the army of Babylon. Nevertheless, the Lord tells Jeremiah to buy a field:

"I bought the field at Anathoth from my cousin Hanamel, and weighed out the money to him, seventeen shekels of silver. I signed the deed, sealed it, got witnesses, and weighed the money on scales. Then I took the sealed deed of purchase, containing the terms and conditions, and the open copy; and I gave the deed of purchase to Baruch, saying, 'Thus says the Lord of hosts, the God of Israel: Take these deeds, both this sealed deed of purchase and this open deed, and put them in an earthenware jar, in order that they may last for a long time. For thus says the Lord of hosts, the God of Israel: 'Houses and fields and vineyards shall again be bought in this land.'"

(Jeremiah 32.9-12, 14-15)

What did Jesus mean by his bit of play-acting? Coming as it did directly before he seized control of the Outer Court of the Temple, the natural interpretation is that it was a condemnation of the unspiritual nature of the Temple authorities. What do you think?

Note: In my account I make play with the name of the village of Bethphage or Beit-Pagey, meaning House of Unripe figs. Of course we do not know if the village was so named before or after the incident with Jesus.

What followed directly was Jesus driving out the money-changers and the traders in sacrificial animals from the temple enclosure. The fig tree re-enters the story the following day.

THE FIG TREE AGAIN

In the morning as they passed by, they saw the fig tree withered away to its roots. Then Peter remembered and said to him, 'Rabbi, look! The fig tree that you cursed has withered.' Jesus answered them, 'Have faith in God. Truly I tell you, if you say to this mountain, "Be taken up and thrown into the sea", and if you do not doubt in your heart, but believe that what you say will come to pass, it will be done for you. So I tell you, whatever you ask for in prayer, believe that you have received it, and it will be yours."

(Mark 11.20-24)

THE SCENE

Yeshua and his followers set out early the next day. After passing through Beit-Pagey, they all noticed the leafless skeleton of a fig tree.

"Look, Rabbi," said Sh'mon Kepha, "that fig tree you cursed yesterday - it's dead! Withered from the ground up! How could that happen?"

Yeshua stopped and contemplated the dead tree, its bare branches pointing like prayer hands into the early morning sky. He looked over his shoulder at his trainees. *"Keep your focus on the Father. Then whatever you say will happen. In fact if you say to that mountain over there,"* he nodded towards the Temple dominating the Kidron valley, *'Be uprooted and thrown into the sea, it will happen."* He smiled at his trainees' dumbfounded expressions, and said, *"Come on, lads, let's go".*

COMMENT

Swami Vivekanda (1863 - 1902), founder of the Hindu Ramakrishna Mission said, *"Think of the power of words."*

Was Jesus surprised that his curse had had such an immediate effect? Perhaps. But not so much. He was aware of the negative power of words: *"I tell you, on the day of judgement you will have to give an account for every careless word you utter; for by your words you will be justified, and by your words you will be condemned."* (Matthew 12.36). And he was aware of their positive power. *"Your faith has healed you. Go in peace."* (Mark 5.34,10.32 Luke 7.50, 8.48 etc.)

A single word can do real harm: *"No one can tame the tongue—a restless evil, full of deadly poison. With it we bless the Lord and Father, and with it we curse those who are made in the likeness of God. From the same mouth come blessing and cursing. My brothers and sisters, this ought not to be so."* (James 3.8-10)

Can a word kill off a tree? I don't know.

And what did Jesus mean when he said: *"If you say to this mountain, "Be taken up and thrown into the sea", and if you do not doubt in your heart, but believe that what you say will come to pass, it will be done for you"?* What was 'this mountain? There was only one mountain in sight, namely the Temple Mount, across the Kidron valley. Was the saying a coded warning of the future destruction of the Temple? Are we as confused as the disciples were?

REFLECTION

Two very difficult passages. No wonder Luke left it out.

However, there are many contemporary examples of prophetic action. The most famous is Greta Thunberg's school strike to wake up world leaders to the crisis of human-created climate change. Other non-violent direct actions have been Greenpeace's two-week's occupation of a new oil rig in the North Sea, the semi-naked protest by Extinction Rebellion in the House of Commons, which I witnessed, and most recently (at the time of writing) Insulate Britain's blockade of the M25.

Would Jesus approve?

SUGGESTION

Psalm 7.11 says:

God is a righteous judge,
and a God who has indignation every day.

Look at the news, either in print or online. What do you think is God's perspective on the various issues?

FRIDAY OF LENT 1 – OCCUPY!

They came to Jerusalem. And Jesus entered the temple and began to drive out those who were selling and those who were buying in the temple, and he overturned the tables of the money-changers and the seats of those who sold doves; and he would not allow anyone to carry anything through the temple. He was teaching and saying, 'Is it not written,

"My house shall be called a house of prayer for all the nations"?
But you have made it a den of robbers.'

(Mark 11.15-17)

THE SCENE

Yeshua strode up the path to the double arched Eastern Gate, past the Temple guards on duty there and out into the Outer Court, followed closely by his twelve trainees. He went up to one of the largest tables on which the currency exchangers bought Roman money and sold ritually pure Temple coinage. The dealer looked up with a slightly shark-like smile at this imposing but clearly unsophisticated new customer.

"Shalom, my friend, how much money do you want to change? You won't get a better rate than mine in the whole of Yerushalayim."

The tall, bearded northerner with piercing eyes just said, *"Get out."*

"Pardon?"

"Out. Out. Out!" With a rapid two-handed lift he tipped the heavy table up, spilling all the silver coins over the Temple floor. He strode over to the next table.

73

"OUT!" he shouted, and tipped that table over too. Soon there was massive confusion with the currency exchangers and the crowd, scrabbling for coins on the marble pavement and other pilgrims joining in the fun.

The Temple guards rushed to the disturbance but were helpless before the manic uproar which now had infected hundreds of the pilgrims. Yeshua took the six pieces of thin rope from his belt and laid about with them right and left, striking cattle, lambs and their owners so that entire Outer Court was filled with shouting and screaming, cattle roaring, sheep baaing, fluttering doves set free from their overturned cages. Too late , the Temple guards realised that they had left all the gateways unattended and that they were now in the hands of burly Galilean pilgrims, looking threateningly pious, and outnumbering the guards two to one.

At each of the gates a traffic jam was developing as traders tried to bring their carts through the Temple as a short cut, only to be met by half a dozen muscled northerners who said, *"You're not going to bring that through here, are you, sunshine?"* And then they couldn't turn round because the cart behind them was blocking their way. It was absolute chaos.

Yeshua stood in the middle of Solomon's Portico and proclaimed:

"Brothers and fathers! You know how Aalah has spoken in the Haftorah, 'My house shall be called a house of prayer for all the Goyim!' The Torah tells us that we are to be a blessing for all the families on earth! But we have allowed the priests to turn this sacred place into a robbers' cave, a den of thieves! And this at Pesach! My brothers and fathers, let us worship

the Holy One, blessed be he, not in mere words, but in spirit and in truth!"

COMMENT

1 Jesus' cleansing of the temple is one of the most famous incidents in his life. The painting by El Greco shows Jesus in a bright pink robe angrily sweeping through the cowering mob of traders like a tornado, a force of nature. Countless sermons have struggled with the nature of Jesus' anger. What is never mentioned is that it was carefully planned.

The late visit to the Temple the previous day was a reconnaissance. In my account, on the day itself Jesus addresses his followers outside the Temple, asking his women followers to stay outside in case there is violence. Which there could easily have been. Either from the Temple guards with their truncheons, or from the Roman troops overlooking the Temple from the Antonia fortress. So the direct action which Jesus took had to be swift and take everyone by surprise. Which it did!

2 Jesus' action was not just a demonstration, an illustration of the prophecies of Isaiah 56.7 and Jeremiah 7.11. It was not a one-off, one day event. It was an occupation!

Mark specifies that *'he would not allow anyone to carry anything through the temple.'* The actual words translated by NRSV as 'anything' actually means containers, in other words trade goods. Quite understandable, because it was quite complicated taking goods east-west through the Jerusalem, and going through the Outer Court of the Temple from the Royal gate to the Eastern Gate was a very useful short cut.

So Jesus had to stop the traffic, much like Insulate Britain did when they blocked the M25. Jesus could only do that by detailing enough burly Galilean pilgrims to be stationed at each of the gates of the Temple, enough to outnumber the temple guards. So it was not a demonstration, it was an occupation.

And it did not last just one day. The next day the authorities ask Jesus "By what authority are you doing these things?" I feel certain that Jesus, with the help of his Galilean supporters, was in charge of the enormous Outer Court of the Temple up to Passover itself.

REFLECTION

Jesus was clearly angry. And it was not just a flash in the pan. His anger had been building since at least his visit to the Temple the day before.

You may have thought that Christians were not supposed to be angry? This is not how we think of the Jesus whom we sing about in hymns:

Jesu, the very thought of thee
with sweetness fills the breast...

When Jesus was confronted with a leper in Mark 1.40-45, we are told he was 'moved with pity' (NRSV). Another and probably original reading is that he was 'moved with anger'. Perhaps against the very nature of leprosy?

When Simon Peter protested that it wasn't right for Jesus to speak of his approaching death, Jesus' riposte was, *"Get behind me , Satan."* (Mark 8.33)

While he was teaching in the Temple, he said, *'Beware of the scribes, who like to walk around in long robes, and to be greeted with respect in the market-places, and to have the best seats in the synagogues and places of honour at banquets! They devour widows' houses and for the sake of appearance say long prayers. They will receive the greater condemnation.'* (Mark 12.38-40)

There is a fierceness about Jesus we would rather avoid. But the New Testament claims that in Jesus we see God himself. *'He is the image of the invisible God, the first-born of all creation."* So if Jesus was fierce, God is too.

How do we cope with a fierce God?

I remember when I was on a long flight to India being challenged by a companion with the question, *'Did God create tigers?'* They are such beautiful creatures, but their ferocity, including their large sharp teeth, is part of their beauty. Is Genesis right when it says that at creation all animals were vegetarian? I don't believe so. I don't believe it because it takes millennia for animals to develop characteristics which able them to survive and flourish, whether to hunt or to escape from hunters. Our world is an amazing balance which if left to itself, as in current re-wilding projects, supports an incredible abundance of different living beings.

It seems to me that God who is the creator of the universe, including the 100 billion stars in our galaxy as well as roughly two trillion galaxies, must be the source of gentleness and ferocity, of beauty and chaos, of creativity and destruction.

In the human life of Jesus of Nazareth we see the same spectrum of compassion and confrontation. He and no other is the one whom the Christian church calls us to follow.

SUGGESTION

I once heard the Dalai Lama speak. It was at a German church festival or Kirchentag, in Munich in 1993. I was struck by one particular thing he said:

"Anger is sometimes useful, hatred never is."

Indeed, Paul in the Letter to the Ephesians actually commands anger:

"Be angry but do not sin; do not let the sun go down on your anger." (Ephesians 4.26)

In other words, express your anger but don't hold on to resentment.

How do we do that? How can we have clean anger? Only by ensuring it is not contaminated with self; with self-pity or self-righteousness or fear. And how do we do that?

First, by praying for those we feel anger against: 'Lord, bless them and give them what they need.' Next, by immersing ourselves in God through meditation and contemplation.

A prayer I say each day is this wonderful Orthodox prayer to the Holy Spirit:

Heavenly King, Comforter, Spirit of truth,
everywhere present, filling all things,
Treasury of good and Giver of life,
come and live in us, and cleanse us from sin,
and of your goodness, heal our souls.

Sit with that for as long as necessary.

SATURDAY OF LENT 1 – CHALLENGING JESUS

The Jews then said to him, 'What sign can you show us for doing this?' Jesus answered them, 'Destroy this temple, and in three days I will raise it up.' The Jews then said, 'This temple has been under construction for forty-six years, and will you raise it up in three days?' But he was speaking of the temple of his body.

(John 2.18-21)

THE SCENE

Some Yerushalayim citizens went up to Yeshua, really angry.

"What are you playing at? You've got no right to act like this, disrupting our Temple. You'd better show us some sign that you've got God on your side - like turning a stick into a snake or water into blood.* Go on, we're waiting."

Yeshua didn't give any ground. He looked intently at the angry group and said,

"You want a sign? All right, here's one. Destroy this temple, and I will raise it up again in three days."

"You're mad! A lunatic - or worse. It's taken forty six years to build this magnificent Temple. You're going to knock it down and rebuild it in three days! You're having a laugh. But you won't last. That's a promise."

* Two of the signs that Moses was told to perform to impress Pharaoh (Exodus 7).

COMMENT

1 This saying of Jesus, recorded by John, is particularly interesting, because it was the basis of one of the accusations against Jesus at his trial before the Sanhedrin, the Jewish Council, in Mark 14.57-59. In other words, it is very likely to have happened.

2 The English translation of Jesus' word "Destroy this temple' is not quite accurate. There are two words that have been translated as temple: 'Hieron', for which we get the word 'hierarchy', and 'naos'. 'Hieron' means the whole temple complex, including the Outer Court. So we are told that Jesus would not allow any trade goods to be carried through the 'hieron'. But that is not the word he used when asked for a sign. This word was 'naos' which means inner shrine or sanctuary. It has a very specific connotation of holiness. So what Jesus actually said was, *"Destroy this shrine and in three days I will raise it up."* It is exactly the same word that Paul uses in 1 Corinthians 6.19 when he says, "Don't you know that your body is a shrine of the Holy Spirit?" The emphasis is not on great buildings. The emphasis is on sacredness. The crowd used the same word as Jesus did, but presumably did not attach the same significance to it.

3 Temples were very different places from their inner shrines. From the Parthenon in Athens to the Rameses II temple at Abu Simbel, from the temple in Jerusalem to the temple devoted to Shiva in Madurai, India, they all followed the same plan. There were open courts where people walked or sat or discussed. These became more enclosed as you travelled towards the centre. Finally there was a small dark room with no windows, where the public was not allowed, the central shrine. In Abu Simbel the shrine has four niches for small statues of four gods, which hardly anyone ever saw. But this dark enclosed space is the spiritual powerhouse of the temple, indeed of the whole community, just as the Holy of Holies was for Israel. The shrine was a secret, sacred space, where darkness and divinity met. This was what Jesus was referring to, and which all our English translations ignore.

REFLECTION

However one interprets the words of Jesus, he was clearly speaking about the future, not something to impress his hearers then and there. It echoes one of my favourite stories of the Old Testament. At the burning bush, Moses says to God, *'Who am I that I should go to Pharaoh, and bring the Israelites out of Egypt?'* He said, *'I will be with you; and this shall be the sign for you that it is I who sent you: when you have brought the people out of Egypt, you shall worship God on this mountain.'* (Exodus 3.11-12)

In my experience that is exactly how God normally works. We follow what seems to be a leading from God, of whatever sort. But it is only in retrospect we can see God's hand subtly at work. As Archbishop William Temple said when asked if prayer works, *"When I pray, coincidences happen, and when I don't, they don't."*

SUGGESTION

Think back along your life. Are there times when things seemed to flow naturally, or even preternaturally, in a way that felt like a fulfilment of your life's journey?

LENT 2

CONFRONTATION

Solomon's Portico

SUNDAY OF LENT 2 – NICODEMUS

Now there was a Pharisee named Nicodemus, a leader of the Jews. He came to Jesus by night and said to him, 'Rabbi, we know that you are a teacher who has come from God; for no one can do these signs that you do apart from the presence of God.'

Jesus answered him, 'Amen amen, I tell you, no one can see the kingdom of God without being born from above.'

Nicodemus said to him, 'How can anyone be born after having grown old? Can one enter a second time into the mother's womb and be born?'

Jesus answered, 'Amen amen, I tell you, no one can enter the kingdom of God without being born of water and Spirit. What is born of the flesh is flesh, and what is born of the Spirit is spirit. Do not be astonished that I said to you, "You must be born from above." The wind blows where it chooses, and you hear the sound of it, but you do not know where it comes from or where it goes. So it is with everyone who is born of the Spirit.'

Nicodemus said to him, 'How can these things be?'

Jesus answered him, 'Are you a teacher of Israel, and yet you do not understand these things? Very truly, I tell you, we speak of what we know and testify to what we have seen; yet you do not receive our testimony. If I have told you about earthly things and you do not believe, how can you believe if I tell you about heavenly things?'

(John 3.1-12)

THE SCENE

I did not include this incident in my book about Jesus' last eight days, because we do not know when it happened. It may have been at an earlier stage of Jesus' life, because

Nicodemus refers to the signs/miracles that Jesus had done. John describes the healing of the cripple at the Pool of Bethesda (John 5), possibly around the feast of tabernacles. The healing of the man born blind (John 9) happened before the feast of Dedication or Hanukkah (John 10.22). But reference to signs could also mean the raising of Lazarus (John 11). This may have happened about February, after which Jesus retreated to a town called Ephraim (John 11.54). Two months later he returned publicly to the Temple. So this conversation could also have happened in Holy Week.

We are told that Nicodemus was a Pharisee, in other words he was meticulous in keeping all the rules of the covenant with God, both written and unwritten. He was also a member of the Sanhedrin, the governing body for Israel under the general supervision of Rome. So he was one of the seventy one most influential people in Israel.

He came to visit Jesus by night. This need not imply that he was afraid, merely that he wanted to talk to Jesus in private. During the day they would both be in the Temple surrounded by thousands of curiosity-seekers.

I imagine he would have made the hour's walk between Jerusalem and Bethany accompanied by a servant for security. Arriving at the house where Jesus and the disciples were staying, he arrived in the main courtyard, and then accompanied Jesus to a small room on one side. There they had their conversation.

Was the talk between Jesus and Nicodemus a private conversation? How did it come to be written down? Did Nicodemus talk about it with John later? We don't know.

COMMENT

1 Amen amen

A notable feature of John's gospel is the frequent use by Jesus of the Hebrew expression 'Amen amen', like a solemn oath, an affirmation of the truth of what follows. All modern translations replace it with 'Very truly' or some such phrase. Archbishop William Temple in his commentary on John said that he regarded this as the actual way Jesus talked. It survived the translation of the words of Jesus not Greek. I think it a shame that it did not survive the translations into English, except in just two versions. I have re-instated it here.

2 Where does it end?

The starting point of the episode is clear. The first verse of the chapter is clearly the beginning. But where did it end? When the gospels were first written there were paragraph breaks, but no chapter divisions or verse numbers, no punctuation, no capital letters (in fact all the letters were upper case up to the 6th century) and no spaces between words. In John 3.1- 21 the passage changes its character half way through. It starts as a straightforward conversation, (Nicodemus saying, *'How can these things be?'*). It ends with straight theological assertions, *(This is the judgement, that the light has come into the world, and people loved darkness rather than light because their deeds were evil).* (John 3.9, 19)

When does it turn from one to the other? Some editions of the Bible give the last words of Jesus as going up to verse 16: *'For God so loved the world that he gave his only Son, so that everyone who believes in him may not perish but may have eternal life.'* Some include verse 13 as part of Jesus' words: *"No one has ascended into heaven except the one who descended from heaven, the Son of Man.'* Others, such as the New Catholic Bible do not. It is a matter for individual judgement. I take the shorter option as being the actual remembered conversation.

3 Pharisees and Charismatics

We see a much more ambiguous relationship between Jesus and the Pharisees in this story. There is a difference in attitude but not an unbridgeable gulf, as there was by the time that the gospel of Matthew came to be written, see Matthew 23. It is only Matthew who calls them 'blind guides' - three times! When writing 'Jesus the Troublemaker', I was struck by how little the Pharisees are mentioned in Jesus' last week. His main attack is directed at the chief priests, scribes and elders. Pharisees were passionate about keeping every detail of the covenant law, both written Torah and that handed down by tradition. Contemporary accounts talk of a more charismatic strain of Judaism, probably centred in Galilee, which fits well into the ministry of Jesus. When Jesus talked about the ministry of the Spirit he was talking from his own experience. He was surprised that this eminent Pharisee had none of that immediate knowledge of God which he took for granted.

REFLECTION

This is a significant passage for me. It produced a light bulb moment in my faith journey. I was in my first year at university and already a Christian, but I knew there was something missing. I went to see a visiting missionary at Worcester College one Saturday morning. The conversation went like this:

"Do you believe in God?"
"Yes"
"Wonderful! And do you believe in Jesus his Son?"
"Yes, I do"
"Excellent. Then all you need is the Holy Spirit."

He then went through John 3, pointing out that 'born again' actually meant 'born from above', being born spiritually. I realised that this meant a radical surrender of myself to the Spirit's direction, and that meant much more serious prayer and Bible study. So on Monday I went to Woolworth's; I bought a rug for the lino floor of my bedroom and an alarm clock. It certainly had a refreshing effect on my faith.

How do we receive the Holy Spirit (or holy spirit - there is usually no definite article)?

The answer is in Luke 11.13:

'If you then, who are evil, know how to give good gifts to your children, how much more will the heavenly Father give the Holy Spirit to those who ask him!'

SUGGESTION

Try this: Sit quietly for some minutes, repeating from time to time the ancient prayer 'Holy Spirit, come to me, kindle in me the fire of your love'.

Or play the Taizé version on YouTube: 'Holy Spirit come to us...'

Or go for a walk and talk to God, as I did, about how I really did not want to surrender my life to the Spirit. That worked too!

MONDAY OF LENT 2 - BY WHAT AUTHORITY?

*A*gain *they came to Jerusalem. As Jesus was walking in the temple, the chief priests, the scribes, and the elders came to him and said, 'By what authority are you doing these things? Who gave you this authority to do them?'.*

(Mark 11.27-28)

THE SCENE

Yeshua took a deep breath, smiled slightly and said, *"That's a fair question. It deserves an answer. I will give you an answer. Providing you answer a question I will ask. You all know Yochanan*, who practised his ministry of baptism not twenty miles from here."* A buzz of recognition rose from the crowd. *"Well now, Yochanan's ministry, was it a call from Adonai Eloheynu** or was it his own idea, a human invention? Tell us."*

The leading priests and Torah-teachers hesitated, looking at each other. *"We need to consult",* said a leading priest, and the delegation withdrew to a quiet corner of the Outer Court.

"We can't say his call was from God. He was a mountebank. Even called us a brood of vipers."

"We're not popular with anyone. We even fight among ourselves. Maybe it's time for us to give some recognition to their Yochanan. After all, he's dead, and it would put the Galilean on the spot."

"But we can't forget his main platform, baptising Jews. We all know what baptism is for. It's what we expect the Goyim, the Gentiles, to do if they want to join the community of Yisrael. And that's right, because they have to give up their

old life and make a brand new start. But this Yochanan called his fellow Jews to be baptised! As if we Israelites were Gentiles! He basically excommunicated everyone who disagreed with him. Including us!"

"We have to be careful. This ignorant crowd all believe that Yochanan was a great prophet. This Yeshua has already used the crowd to kick the perfectly legal traders out of the Temple. He could turn them against us in a flash. It's just too dangerous."

The group of leading priests, Torah-teachers and Council members walked back to Yeshua with as much dignity as they could muster.

"Well, gentlemen, what is your answer?"

"We have considered carefully, and have decided that there are so many issues at stake, that we can't make a definitive statement at this moment."

"Then neither will I tell you what my authority is for standing up for the holiness of this place."

* John
** Lord our God

COMMENT

1 This is such a wonderful dramatic scene. The chief priests were of course quite right to challenge this northerner who had taken over most of the Temple area. The way that Jesus slips out of answering a straightforward question is sheer genius. In the discussion among the Temple authorities I have expressed what I believe was the radical nature of John's preaching. It was a message which Jesus shared, as he (or his disciples) continued baptising people themselves for some time (John 3.22).

2 What were the differences between Jews and the rest of the Roman world? First, Jews insisted that there was only one God, not multiple gods.

Then, Jews had the Torah which specified much of the way one lived, including, crucially only eating kosher food. The rest of society happily ate meat from the meat market, most of which would have been offered as a sacrifice to various pagan gods.

Finally, Jews were very suspicious of the various sexual practices of the ancient world, whether homosexuality among the Greeks or the many licensed brothels.
Being baptised meant abandoning a lot of what your friends and neighbours thought was perfectly normal.

3 Behind this encounter was the fact that the Sadducees, the group the chief priest belonged to, were very unpopular. Josephus, in his 'Jewish War' said,

'Sadducees, even towards each other, show a more disagreeable spirit, and in their relations with men like themselves they are as harsh as they might be towards foreigners.'

A leading Pharisee, Yochanan ben Zakkai, said, *'Guard your steps when you go to the house of God. To draw near to listen is better than to offer the sacrifice of fools, for they do not know they are doing evil.'* Pretty damning.

REFLECTION

How often we find ourselves put on the spot by someone and can't think of a response. So the other person wins by default. Then half an hour later we think of the perfect reply! I can think of only one occasion when I managed to respond effectively at the time. In the mid-1970's I was Acting Personnel Officer at Hammersmith Hospital. The Hospital Secretary, Mr Adams, called me to his office. When I entered, he asked,

"Mr Roland, do you think it's a good thing for you to be somewhat eccentric?"

"Do you mean my beard?" (I had quite an impressive beard at that time).

"No, no that's fine. It's just been commented that you often come to work on a bicycle."

Without thinking, I simply said,

"Oh no, love me, love my bike."

He could not think of an answer and I left.

That response did not come from normal thinking brain, it came from a deeper level of consciousness, a direct awareness of my self. Jesus was clearly so at one with himself that these instant responses came naturally, to the intense annoyance of his opponents.

How can we tap into the kind of awareness and acceptance of ourselves that will allow us to respond in the moment? Jesus said, "Truly I tell you, whoever does not receive the kingdom of God as a little child will never enter it." (Mark

10.15). Being in touch with our inner child, welcoming the spirit of play into our lives, is how we relearn the skill we had in childhood of living spontaneously.

SUGGESTION

Do something just for fun.

TUESDAY OF LENT 2 - A POINTED STORY

*T*hen Jesus began to speak to them in parables. 'A man planted
a vineyard, put a fence around it, dug a pit for the wine press,
and built a watch-tower; then he leased it to tenants and went to
another country... Finally he sent his son to them, saying, "They
will respect my son." But those tenants said to one another, "This
is the heir; come, let us kill him, and the inheritance will be ours."
So they seized him, killed him, and threw him out of the vineyard.
What then will the owner of the vineyard do? He will come and
destroy the tenants and give the vineyard to others'.

(Mark 12.1, 6-9)

THE SCENE

Yeshua's gaze shifted to include the whole of the crowd
that had gathered.

"I have a story to tell you."

Instantly the crowd became quiet and attentive. The
priests and Council members were trapped there in
front of Yeshua.

*"There was a once a rich man, living in Cyprus, who bought
up an estate in the land of Y'hudah.*

A hiss of anger rose from the crowd.

*"This man sent his steward over to organise the construction
of a vineyard during the winter months. He hired local
farmers at the minimum wage to do the work. Then the
steward hired four of these local farmers to keep an eye on
things and make sure that some wine got produced in three
years' time.*

"The tenants didn't have much to do at first, so they planted some onions, leeks and cucumbers. Then in the autumn, a man came who said he'd come from the owner in Cyprus, who wanted his cut. Well, as you can guess, they sent him away with a flea in his ear!

The crowd chuckled at the farmers' chutzpah.

"The absentee landowner didn't blame his servant. He just said, "Maybe they didn't realise you went on my say-so. We'll try again next year."

"Next year another servant came and showed a letter from the landowner. He asked for a fifth of the profit from the vegetables the farmers had harvested. The tenant-farmers got angry and he also retreated back to Cyprus.

"The next autumn, the owner's son said, 'Listen father, let me go. They will recognise me, and now that there will be some grapes, there is no reason for them to refuse to give us some return on our investment.'

'Perhaps you're right,' the father said, 'Go, but be careful.'

"The son arrived at the village. It was clear who he was, not only because of his father's signet ring. There was some argument over how much of the grapes were the land-owner's property. That night, the tenant-farmers got together. 'Why did this guy come instead of another servant? Do you think the old man's died? After all, he's got his signet ring. And if the old man is dead, this guy is the heir! If something happened to him, the vineyard would have no owner, and it'd be first come, first served. We'd be sitting pretty!'

"Next day, when the son came to conclude negotiations, one of the farmers brought a large rock crashing down on the *back of his head. They took his body and threw it on the side of the road outside the vineyard, as if he had been killed by brigands. But that deceived nobody."*

The crowd shifted uncomfortably at the story's harsh ending.

"So - what do you think the rich man in Cyprus will do when he hears about it?"

"He'll get soldiers and kill those farmers," said someone in the crowd. *"And then he'll let out the vineyard to some honest men."*

"I think so," said Yeshua. He looked directly at the delegation in front of him. *"The vineyard-keepers will be replaced."*

The group of leading priests, Torah-teachers and Council members were dumb-founded at the sudden attack. Yeshua spoke again.

"Perhaps you have never read or understood what is written in the Readings.*

*'The stone that the builders rejected
has become the chief cornerstone."*

A Council member whispered to one of the leading priests, *"Why don't you get the Temple guards to arrest him?"*

The priest whispered back. *"Not the right time. Don't worry, his time will come."*

* The Hebrew Scriptures that were read publicly in the synagogue. Later called the Tanakh - law, prophets, writings.

COMMENT

1 The story of the vineyard tenants is a curious one. The ideas behind my interpretation come from the excellent German Biblical scholar Jeremias. The background is of economic exploitation, similar to today's globalisation, in which wealthy individuals and corporations from outside take over the land, reducing formerly independent farmers to the status of day-labourers. So at the start of the story, the land-owner is in fact a villain. No one in Jesus' audience could guess how it would end. The violence and the turning of the vineyard tenants into the villains must have come as complete shock to them, and to the chief priests.

2 Jesus had a knack of using disreputable characters to represent God, whether a burglar (Mark 3.27), a forgetful housewife (Luke 15.8-10) or a grumpy neighbour (Luke 11.5-8). The absentee landowner is one more instance.

REFLECTION

At one level the story is about entitlement. The rich man in Cyprus felt entitled to the normal 'cut' from the profits of the grapes and wine, and before that was ready, of the vegetables that were grown. The tenants felt entitled to some benefit for all the hard work they had put in, over and above the regular wages (not large) they would have received. When the son and heir arrived, they felt entitled to make a bid for the ownership of the vineyard. After all they were the native residents there.

In Jesus' audience the chief priests felt entitled to the power and prestige that came with their position, their family, their tradition.

The problem with entitlement is that you put blinkers on yourself, like blinkers on horses which stops them see anything to the side. If all you see is your entitlement, you become blind to the effect you have on other people, particularly on those less fortunate than yourself.

Of course Jesus was pointing out how the tenants, because of their blinkered sense of entitlement, were making a very serious mistake and were bringing down destruction on their heads. The implicit lesson being that that was just what the temple establishment was doing in treating him as a nuisance to be got rid of instead of as God's final appeal to Israel to come back to him.

SUGGESTION

Read Psalm 118.

See how many verses seem to prefigure the last hours of Jesus' life and what followed.

WEDNESDAY OF LENT 2 – BEWARE OF LAWYERS

'*Beware of the scribes, who like to walk around in long robes, and to be greeted with respect in the market-places, and to have the best seats in the synagogues and places of honour at banquets! They devour widows' houses and for the sake of appearance say long prayers. They will receive the greater condemnation.*'

(Mark 12.38-40)

COMMENT

1 When was this said?

This somewhat aggressive speech comes at the end of Jesus' teaching in Mark 12. It is introduced with the general phrase, 'as he taught, he said...' with no other time indication. In 'Jesus the Troublemaker' I placed it immediately after yesterday's story of the vineyard tenants, because the scribes were one of the groups whom Jesus targeted in that story, namely the chief priests, scribes and elders (Mark 11.27).

2 Who were the chief priests, scribes and elders?

In my book the chief priests are called leading priests and sometimes Temple aristocrats. They were members of a tight-knit group of powerful families, some but not all of priestly descent, hand-in-glove with the prevailing political power.

The elders would have been some of the seventy one members of the Sanhedrin, or Great Council, who were responsible for the regular government of Israel, including deciding on the dates of the major temple festivals.

The scribes I called Torah-teachers in my book. Their function was much greater than simply writing things down. They were the experts in the Law, specifically the

100

Torah, the first five books, which included all the worship regulations for the temple. They were religious lawyers, part of the temple establishment. (See Mark 7.1). They were also present in all the communities of Israel. When Jesus said to the paralysed man in Carpernaum, *"Your sins are forgiven",* it was the scribes who questioned, *"Why does this fellow speak in this way? It is blasphemy!"* (Mark 2.7)

There were also a great number of priests, so many that they had to determine by lot who should take part in the various daily duties in the temple, see Luke 1.8. They were outside the regular power structures. Luke comments that eventually a great many of them 'became obedient to the faith'. (Acts 6.7)

REFLECTION

What was Jesus' primary accusation against the scribes? It was not that they were corrupt and greedy - though that comes in as a secondary assertion. It was that their prime motivation was to look good in the eyes of society - to be given the best seats at banquets or synagogues, to be treated with great respect in public.

Well, isn't that nice? Don't we all want to have a good reputation, to be quoted approvingly in the media, to have the most Facebook followers? What's wrong with that?

The principal danger is that a by-product of gaining the whole world is that we can lose our souls, the best part of ourselves. Politics is a prime arena for this. I once knew a former serjeant-at-arms of the House of Commons who commented that after a general election the new members of parliament come in full of ideals, but after about six months they had become like all of the rest. I remember when Michael Portillo, Secretary of Defence, lost his seat in an astonishing upset at the 1997 election. He had been widely disliked. The loss of his seat resulted in an astonishing transformation, which included taking part in a television programme in 2002 in which he spent a week in the shoes of a single mother looking after a family on benefits in Wallasey; (he didn't quite make it). Sometimes it takes a hard knock to teach us proper humility; to see ourselves in a realistic perspective alongside other people with different life experiences; to find our true selves.

And of course if you use your position to feather your own nest, that makes you even more culpable. Sadly, that is all too common a trait among top politicians all over the world.

SUGGESTION

Make a list of those people who know us well, outside our immediate family. Is there a discernible pattern? Is there something we could do to expand our circle of acquaintances? Such as helping at a food bank, or visiting a church in a different part of town, or going to a church with a different racial mix? A model example for me was when I visited St Stephen Wallbrook. One churchwarden was an investment banker, the other was a cleaning lady.

THURSDAY OF LENT 2 – THE QUESTION OF TAXES

They sent to him some Pharisees and some Herodians to trap him in what he said. And they came and said to him, 'Teacher, we know that you are sincere, and show deference to no one; for you do not regard people with partiality, but teach the way of God in accordance with truth. Is it lawful to pay taxes to the emperor, or not? Should we pay them, or should we not?' But knowing their hypocrisy, he said to them, 'Why are you putting me to the test? Bring me a denarius and let me see it.' And they brought one. Then he said to them, 'Whose head is this, and whose title?' They answered, 'The emperor's.' Jesus said to them, 'Give to the emperor the things that are the emperor's, and to God the things that are God's.' And they were utterly amazed at him.

(Mark 12.13-17)

THE SCENE

The gospels give the story in a few masterly brush-strokes. They omit the reaction of the crowd. Here is how I imagined it.

> The crowd began to dispute excitedly. *"Of course it's wrong, we are the free people of the Lord!" "We've got no choice, they've got their soldiers here, even looking down on us right now from the Antonia". "How can we bear being in subjection to the Goyim?" "But we're free to worship, and they allow us raise taxes from Jews in the Dispersion to support the Temple."*
>
> *"You can't make money more important than freedom!"*

Yeshua regarded the group of Hasidim and Liberals, as well as the excited crowd with an ironic eye.

"My friends, you have asked a hard question. You'll have to help me a bit. Have any of you got a denarius on you?"

"Yes, rabbi," said one, handing it up.

Yeshua took it and examined it carefully. The crowd grew silent in anticipation.

"Todah lak" he said, handing it back. *"Tell me, what does the inscription say?"*

"Caesar Augustus."

"And whose image is on the coin?"

"Caesar Augustus."

"Then give to Caesar what belongs to Caesar, and to Aalah* what belongs to Aalah."

*Aramaic for 'God'

COMMENT

1 Who were the Pharisees?

The Pharisees, the ones who 'separated themselves', had been active since 160 BCE, in bitter and sometimes bloody rivalry with the Sadducees. They were committed to keeping all the rules of the Torah, both written and unwritten, those in the Torah itself and those handed down in oral tradition, 613 in all. But they interpreted the Law in a way that made sense to people. For instance, when the law said 'an eye for an eye', they said the punishment could be commuted to a money fine. The Sadducees said you had to take out the forfeited eye. The Pharisees hoped that one day all of Israel would keep the Law perfectly and then the Messiah would come.

Josephus writing about 90 CE, gave the number of Pharisees as 6,000, and said they were the most highly regarded teachers by the common people. After the Temple was destroyed in 70 AD, they were the only Jewish group to survive. The later rabbis were their successors. They effectively created the Judaism we know today.

2 Where were the Pharisees

Where were they during Jesus' last eight days? Apart from today's challenge they do not figure at all in Mark's account of Holy Week and only once in Luke's. Their absence is striking. Jesus' attack is primarily on the Temple authorities, the chief priests and the scribes. There was tension between Jesus and the Pharisees, as in Luke 11.37-53, but there were noteworthy exceptions: Nicodemus, and some members of the early church in Jerusalem (Acts 15.5)

But Matthew is different. He has a long passage denouncing the Pharisees and scribes, almost the whole of chapter 23, plus the two preceding passages. Matthew also includes the 'blood libel' of the crowd in Matthew 27.25, 'his blood be on us and on our children'. This has been the seedbed of two thousand years of Christian anti-semitism. Perhaps it should be relegated to an appendix.

3 Who were the Herodians?

Mark is the only ancient writer to mention the Herodians. They were clearly supporters of Herod Antipas, who had ruled Galilee and part of Transjordan (Peraea) for the last thirty five years. His main policy seems to have been to keep the peace and to help the economy. His building of two major cities, Sepphoris and Tiberias did that, but at the cost of displeasing the devout, because Tiberias, while providing a major source of employment, was built partly over a disused cemetery. He was careful not to offend Jewish sensibilities so had image-free coinage. However, keeping the peace also included imprisoning and ultimately executing John the Baptist and trying to get hold of Jesus. In my book I refer to Herodians as Liberals, similar to Liberal Judaism today, which seeks to make a sensible accommodation between traditional Judaism and the modern world.

4 Where did this story take place?

The only other place where Herodians are mentioned are in Mark 3.1-3, the story of the healing of the man with the withered hand in the synagogue, presumably the synagogue at Capernaum. And yet it is beyond doubt that today's story took place in Jerusalem. Had it been in Galilee the denarius would not have had Caesar's head and inscription on it.

REFLECTION

The question put to Jesus is a clever way of putting someone on the spot. *"Is it right to pay taxes to Caesar or not?"* It was not possible to give an answer that would not get Jesus into trouble, either with the Roman occupying power if he said 'no', or with the ordinary people, if he said yes. Jesus first plays for time, just a few seconds thinking time.

Jesus' reply is masterly. *"Give to Caesar what is Caesar's, and give to God what is God's"*. It seems to answer the question completely, and yet it is very ambiguous. Does it mean, pay your taxes? Or, if Israel is God's possession, is it a covert call for armed insurrection (as I have seen it argued). Or does it mean, *"I am not bothered"?*

Those thirteen words hold a depth and an authority that puts our day-to-day lives under a microscope. They are a litmus test for our daily actions and reactions. There are those who have legitimate authority over us; and there is God's call on us to stand up for the values of his kingdom.

These words maintain the proper duty we have to political authority; and the right to withstand that authority when it clashes with our duty to God and with the well-being of our fellow men and women.

We are never going to get it quite right; and today's right answer may be tomorrow's wrong one. Ultimately Jesus' saying is a call for us to be in constant dialogue with God, our neighbours and the powers-that-be. It is a call to pray and to work.

SUGGESTION

Draw three overlapping circles.
In one, write your responsibilities to society.
In a second, write your responsibilities to God
In a third, write your personal responsibilities.

What would you put in the overlapping section? That may be your primary calling.

FRIDAY OF LENT 2 - RESURRECTION?

Some Sadducees, who say there is no resurrection, came to him and asked saying, 'Teacher, Moses wrote for us that if a man's brother dies, leaving a wife but no child, the man shall marry the widow and raise up children for his brother. There were seven brothers; the first married and, when he died, left no children; and the second married her and died, and the third likewise; down to the seventh. Now, in the resurrection whose wife will she be? For the seven had married her.'

Jesus said to them, 'Is not this the reason you are wrong, that you know neither the scriptures nor the power of God? For when they rise from the dead, they neither marry nor are given in marriage, but are like angels in heaven... You are quite wrong.'

(Mark 12.18-27, ed.)

THE SCENE

There was a stir in the crowd as an impressive group of Temple aristocrats made their away towards Yeshua, their lavishly embroidered coats and turbans making a striking contrast with the simple brown cloak worn by Yeshua. The crowd settled into a resentful silence.

"Rabbi, we have a case which we would like your opinion on," said the leading Temple aristocrat.

"Go on," said Yeshua.

"In the Torah, Moshe laid down this rule:

'When brothers reside together, and one of them dies and has no son, the wife of the deceased shall not be married outside the family to a stranger. Her husband's brother shall go in to her, taking her in marriage, and performing the duty of a

husband's brother to her, and the firstborn whom she bears shall succeed to the name of the deceased brother, so that his name may not be blotted out of Israel.'

"Now just this happened among us. There were seven brothers, and the eldest married a woman, but he died before she could conceive.

"Then the second brother married the woman, and he died before she conceived."

Then the third brother married her, but he died too. The fourth brother's funeral was just a few days after the wedding. The fifth brother lasted longer but again the woman had no children to carry on the family name. The sixth brother fared no better. And the seventh also perished without any children. In the end, the woman herself died."

"About time too!"

"Worn out, was she?" A guffaw of laughter came from the back of the crowd.

"Now, Rabbi, your judgement please. In the so-called resurrection, which you and the Hasidim believe in so devoutly, whose wife will she be? All seven of the brothers had had her."

A buzz of hilarity and curiosity issued from the crowd.

Yeshua's face showed not a hint of humour.

"Isn't this why you aristocrats go so wrong? You think you revere the Torah, but you haven't even begun to understand it. You have no clue about either the Readings or the power of Aalah. When men and women rise from the dead, they

109

neither marry nor are given in marriage. They are like the messengers whom Aalah sends out, spiritual beings in the life beyond.

And as for the dead being raised, haven't you even read the Torah itself? How in the passage about the burning bush, Aalah said to him, 'I am Elohim of Avraham, and Elohim of Yitzchak, and Elohim of Ya'akov.'. He is not Elohim of the dead but of the living. You are quite wrong."

The crowd burst into applause.

The Temple aristocrats grimaced, then angrily shouldered their way out of the crowd. One muttered, *"You see? Just another of these new-fangled rabble-rousers. No learning. No respect for tradition."*

Note: The Torah is the first five books of the Hebrew Scriptures, from Genesis to Deuteronomy, the foundation of the Jewish religion.

Aalah is the Aramaic word for God.

Elohim is the Hebrew name for God
Hasidim, modern Orthodox Jews, is the word I use instead of Pharisees.

The Readings are the Hebrew Scriptures which were read publicly in the synagogue. It was later called the Tanakh, short for Law, Prophets, Writings.

COMMENT

1 Where did this happen?
We are told that Jesus preached in Solomon's portico, the enormous colonnade on the eastern side of the Temple,

where the early church were later to meet regularly (Acts 5.12). It is likely that this is where this discussion took place.

2 Who were the Sadducees?

The Sadducees were the top layer of society in Israel. They took their name from the first high priest of Solomon's temple, Zadok. It was only after the return from exile in Babylon in the 6th century BCE that the temple became the centre of Jewish society as well as its religious heart. The senior priestly families thus became the rulers of Israel as well as the chief priests. From the time of Herod I, the high priests, though changed at will by the political rulers, were all drawn from the same family. Hence the name I give them, 'Temple aristocrats'.

3 What did the Sadducees believe?

Sadducees were often in dispute with the Pharisees, because they took only the written Torah as authoritative and would have nothing to do with the developing Pharisaic oral tradition. In particular they rejected the Pharisees' belief in the after life and in the resurrection from the dead. So when Paul was on trial before the Sanhedrin, in order to divide his accusers, he cried out, *"I am on trial concerning the hope of the resurrection of the dead."* (Acts 23.7-10)

4 Jesus' argument

Angels:

Jesus comes down squarely on the Pharisees' side of the argument. First he says quite clearly that those who die in God are *'like angels"*. That does not mean they have wings. Wings do not feature in any of the accounts of angels in the Bible except in a few passages in the Book of Revelation. Rather, they are *"spirits in the divine service, sent to serve for the sake of those who are to inherit salvation."* (Hebrews 1.14). When people encounter them they are presumably in the likeness of ordinary people. When the angel Gabriel

111

appeared to Mary and said to her, *"Greetings, favoured one! The Lord is with you,"* we are told that Mary was much perplexed by his words - not by his wings!

'Like angels' clearly indicates that life after death is not simply an action replay of our present life. Paul reflects wisely on this when he says, *But someone will ask, 'How are the dead raised? With what kind of body do they come? ... What is sown is perishable, what is raised is imperishable. It is sown in dishonour, it is raised in glory. It is sown in weakness, it is raised in power. It is sown a physical body, it is raised a spiritual body.'* (1 Corinthians 15.35, 42-44)

God:
Jesus quotes a passage at the very heart of the Torah, Exodus 3.6, the Lord's encounter with Moses at the burning bush. God is clearly beyond death. So if he calls himself the God of Abraham, Isaac and Jacob, they too in consequence are beyond death.

REFLECTION

At last, an answer!

We have already encountered Jesus' clever ways of dealing with disputes, by a counter question or by an enigmatic story. This is one of the very few times he gives a straight answer. Indeed, he says to the Sadducees, *"You are quite wrong."* The Sadducees didn't believe his answer. Do we?

Dare we believe it on behalf of those we love who have died?
Dare we believe it on our own account?
Does it change the way we see the injustices and sufferings of the world?

SUGGESTION

This passage is very rarely used at funerals. Why do you
think that is? What would you like at your own funeral?

SATURDAY OF LENT 2 – WHOSE SON?

While Jesus was teaching in the temple, he said, 'How can the scribes say that the Messiah is the son of David? David himself, by the Holy Spirit, declared,

"The Lord said to my Lord,
'Sit at my right hand,
until I put your enemies under your feet.'"
David himself calls him Lord; so how can he be his son?'

And the large crowd was listening to him with delight.

(Mark 12.35-37)

THE SCENE

This is an isolated saying, part of Jesus' teaching in the temple over a period of four days. It gives a flavour of the back-and-forth nature of Jesus' teaching, more like being on a soap box at Speakers Corner in Hyde Park than standing six feet above criticism in a church pulpit.

COMMENT

What is the point for this little piece of teaching? Is Jesus saying that the standard prophecies of the Messiah in the Old Testament don't apply to him, such as being born in Bethlehem? Is he downgrading David, the great hero of the kingdom of Israel?

The clue lies in his previous attacks on the scribes, the religious lawyers of Jerusalem. He is in fact defending his ministry against the attacks from the religious establishment: *"Why does this fellow speak in this way? It is blasphemy! Who can forgive sins but God alone?"* (Mark 2.7). What Jesus does is introduce a topic that should be as easy for them to discuss as ABC: Whose son is the Messiah? He then asks them a question they can't answer. In other words these eminent lawyers can't answer a basic question about the national hope. They are indeed *'blind guides'* (Matthew 15.14).

REFLECTION

From 'The Importance of Being Ernest' by Oscar Wilde:

Lady Bracknell: *I have always been of opinion that a man who desires to get married should know either everything or nothing. Which do you know?*

Jack: [After some hesitation.] *I know nothing, Lady Bracknell.*

Lady Bracknell: *I am pleased to hear it. I do not approve of anything that tampers with natural ignorance. Ignorance is like a delicate exotic fruit; touch it and the bloom is gone. The whole theory of modern education is radically unsound.*

It is of course a joke. But there is a small point in it. Writing to the General Assembly of the Church of Scotland in 1650, Oliver Cromwell said, *"I beseech you, in the bowels of Christ, think it possible you may be mistaken."* When we say, *"I know I'm right"*, not only does it cut off any discussion, it also takes away the possibility of learning from someone you have already decided you disagree with. The key is to say *"I think I'm right"*, but not, *"I know I'm right."* All of us think we're right - obviously, or we wouldn't think it. But none of us know we're right. In fact we all live in the twilight of knowledge, and new light can break out from the most unexpected places.

To maintain a rigid position indicates not faith but fear. Religions are one of the prime sources of such rigidity - but

115

also of the faith that liberates people to be truly themselves. I think that Jesus came to liberate us from fear (among other things).

From what we read in the gospels, the scribes took a predetermined position towards Jesus based on their reading of the Torah. But what if something greater than the Torah was here?

SUGGESTION

Think of someone you disagree with. Write down the points of disagreement, then those points where you agree, and finally the points they make that make you think.

SHADOWS OF THE STORM

The Mount of Olives c. 1900

SUNDAY OF LENT 3 – THE GOLDEN RULE

*O*ne of the scribes came near and heard them disputing with one another, and seeing that he answered them well, he asked him, 'Which commandment is the first of all?'

Jesus answered, 'The first is, "Hear, O Israel: the Lord our God, the Lord is one; you shall love the Lord your God with all your heart, and with all your soul, and with all your mind, and with all your strength." The second is this, "You shall love your neighbour as yourself." There is no other commandment greater than these.'

Then the scribe said to him, 'You are right, Teacher; you have truly said that "he is one, and besides him there is no other"; and "to love him with all the heart, and with all the understanding, and with all the strength", and "to love one's neighbour as oneself", – this is much more important than all whole burntofferings and sacrifices.'

When Jesus saw that he answered wisely, he said to him, 'You are not far from the kingdom of God.'

After that no one dared to ask him any question.

(Mark 12.28-34)

THE SCENE

A Torah-teacher in the crowd, easily identified by his long-sleeved tunic and black cloak, pushed his way forward.

"Rabbi, I have heard your discussion with our friends the Temple aristocrats. May I be permitted to put a question to you?"

"Surely"

"What then is the first commandment in all the Torah? How do you read it?"

Yeshua stood up straight with his arms outstretched and recited, *"The first commandment is, 'Shema, Yisrael, Adonai Eloheynu, Adonai echad, and you shall love Adonai Eloheynu with all your heart and with all your soul and with all your mind, and with all your strength.' The second is this, 'You shall love your neighbour as yourself." No other commandment is greater than these."*

COMMENT

1 If there is one story about Jesus that almost certainly historical it is this one. The religious lawyer comes out in a particularly good light. Matthew treats him as a hostile witness, and specifies that he was a Pharisee, one of Matthew's least favourite people.

Here the Torah-teacher is actually more radical than Jesus. He says that the two greatest commandments are *'much more important than all whole burnt-offerings and sacrifices'*, the whole business of the Temple where they are standing. This is a clear strand in the teaching of the Old Testament prophets, but never articulated as such by Jesus.

2 Christian preachers sometimes speak of the genius of Jesus in summarising the demands of the Torah so well. In fact Jesus was simply proclaiming what every Jew recited when he prayed, the ABC of the Jewish religion: Deuteronomy 6.6-9, followed by Leviticus 18. The great rabbi Hillel (1st century BCE) was once asked to recite the whole Torah while standing on one leg. He said, *"What is hateful to* *you, do not do to your fellow: this is the whole Torah; the rest is commentary; go and learn."*

3 I once heard a rabbi expound the Shema (Hebrew for Hear!). What does it mean to say that the Lord our God is one? The word one, or 'echad', is very emphatic.

First, it means that God is not many - there are not multiple divinities each responsible for their own little bit of the world.

Second, he is not three - i.e Jesus is not a second god nor the Holy Spirit a third. Christian-speak can all too easily fall into the habit of talking just like that. Michael Ramsey, former Archbishop of Canterbury, was once asked if there was a book which summarised all the different Christian heresies. *"Oh yes,"* he replied, *"it's called Hymns Ancient and Modern."*

Third, he is not two. There are not two equal and opposite spiritual forces in the universe the good spirit and the evil spirit. This was the belief of Zoroastrianism which was the religion of the Persian empire up to the coming of Islam. It still survives as the faith of Parsees in India. Some Christians make the devil almost equal to God. I was shocked to hear a very respected evangelical leader commenting in 1984 on the death from cancer of the evangelist David Watson. I heard him say from the pulpit, *"The devil won."*

Fourth, he is not none. The world is not self-explanatory. There is a mystery at the heart of all things, as well as a mystery in the human heart, a mystery which ultimately binds all things in unity. When we address ourselves to God, we are doing something meaningful.

4 The kingdom of God

Whole libraries have been written about Jesus' use of the phrase 'kingdom of God'. What did Jesus mean when he told the scribe he was not far from the kingdom?

a. It was a compliment. He was not saying, *"Nearly is not quite, sorry, you've missed the bus."*

b. In 'Jesus the Troublemaker' Jesus says, *"You are not far from Aalah's kingly rule."* When I was studying theology at Durham I spent two whole weeks struggling with what Jesus meant. The most helpful book for me was 'Jesus and the Kingdom of God' by G R Beasley-Murray. His view was the kingdom was a dynamic concept, referring to activity, not to a static image with set boundaries. 'God's kingly rule' is in my view wherever God is actively at work defeating evil. My summary phrase would be 'God at work'.

c. What does it mean to be *'not far from Aalah's kingly rule'?* It's where we all are, once we surrender our lives to God. We are always on the threshold. It is God who takes the initiative in ways that can surprise us, even in retrospect. As the Alcoholics Anonymous slogan goes, *'Coincidences are God's way of remaining anonymous."*

REFLECTION

Jesus quoted just the first line of the Shema. The full Shema, Deuteronomy 6.6-9, recited at least daily, goes like this:

'Hear, O Israel: The Lord is our God, the Lord is one. You shall love the Lord your God with all your heart, and with all your soul, and with all your might.

'Keep these words that I am commanding you today in your heart. Recite them to your children and talk about them when you are at home and when you are away, when you lie down and when you rise. Bind them as a sign on your hand, fix them as an emblem on your forehead, and write them on the doorposts of your house and on your gates.

It means constantly reminding ourselves of God and his call on our lives. Faith is not a Sunday morning only occupation. Nor even a daily morning prayer occupation. It can inform our whole lives. Reciting simple prayers can be the background music of our day.

In the luminous little book, 'The Way of the Pilgrim', an anonymous 19th century Russian Christian recounts how his heart was transformed by saying the Jesus prayer constantly: "Lord Jesus Christ, Son of God, have mercy upon me, a sinner." It can be shortened to 'Lord Jesus, have mercy', or just to 'Jesus'.

It can be particularly helpful when we are doing something boring or when we are waiting for a bus. When I was working in a factory I used to use the first half of the Jesus prayer while unscrewing a screw and the second half while screwing it up.

Alcoholics Anonymous, that remarkable spiritual guide, advises that we *say many times a day, "Thy will be done."*

One of the Desert Fathers, monks in Egypt in the 4th century, was asked by another monk, "I say my prayers, I fast regularly, I keep my thoughts chaste, what else should I do?" The Abba replied, "If you will, you can become all flame."

SUGGESTION

Choose one of the following simple prayers and try to keep returning to it in the course of your day:

"Lord Jesus Christ, Son of God, have mercy upon me, a sinner."

I sometimes use the word 'rebel' instead - it's true for me. Or I shorten it simply to 'Lord Jesus' or to 'Jesus'.

Your will, not mine, be done.

Abba Father, Jesus Lord, Spirit of God, Alleluia

Or if you want to try it in Hebrew (the 'ch' is pronounced as in the Scottish 'loch'):

Abba Eloheynu, Yeshua Adonai, Ruach ha-kodesh. Hallujah

MONDAY OF LENT 3 - THE WIDOW'S MITE

Jesus sat down opposite the treasury, and watched the crowd putting money into the treasury. Many rich people put in large sums. A poor widow came and put in two small copper coins, which are worth a penny. Then he called his disciples and said to them, 'Truly I tell you, this poor widow has put in more than all those who are contributing to the treasury. For all of them have contributed out of their abundance; but she out of her poverty has put in everything she had, all she had to live on.'

Mark 12.41-44)

THE SCENE

Yeshua sat down next to the one of the thirteen big trumpet-shaped bronze donation boxes. Many wealthy men and women in highly-coloured striped and chequered cloaks came and theatrically tossed gold and silver coins into the metal mouths. Yeshua was idly watching everything going on. Suddenly he stiffened.

"See her?" he asked his group of trainees.

"Who?" "Which one?"

"That woman walking away, with the black cloak and shawl. The widow. I saw how much she put into the treasury box. Two farthings," he said admiringly.

"Two farthings? That's not much!"

"On the contrary. It's more than all the rest put in. Everyone else gave what they could afford. She gave what she couldn't afford, all that she had to live on. You may not have seen it, but the Holy One, blessed be he, certainly did."

The silver trumpets signalled the start of the evening sacrifice and Yeshua and his group stood up to pray. At the end of the prayers they made their way out through the North Gate.

COMMENT

This is not the favourite story of hard-working vicars. When you need to pay the the diocesan quota, the heating bills and the organist, a couple of pence doesn't go very far. We do of course pay lip-service to the idea that it's the heart that counts, not the amount. But it doesn't get the bills paid.

And yet.... When I was a member of St Jude's Courtfield Gardens, Earls Court, and still a Personnel Officer, there was an elderly lady in our congregation who would put 10p. into the collection each week. It wan't much even then. But I found out that she lived-in a residential home nearby and was given a spending allowance of £1 per week. 10p was 10% of her disposable income - a tithe. I was impressed.

So what should Christians give? A standard amount enshrined in the Old Testament is a tenth or a tithe. There is nothing laid down in the New Testament, the only instruction is that our giving should be cheerful. However, because we are weak and fallible creatures, a general rule on this matter is helpful.

I once met a former South African journalist who had escaped from the apartheid regime in a rowing boat. He found a home here in the UK with the Franciscans. His rule of thumb was to give a tenth of his disposable income, giving it in line with Jesus summary of the Law which we considered yesterday, namely half to the work of God and half to our needy neighbour.

That has always struck me as a sensible approach: to give 5% of my disposable income, after tax and rent/mortgage, to my local church, and 5% to charities helping those in need worldwide. Of course, as C S Lewis rather frighteningly said, a tenth should be just the starting-off point of our giving.

REFLECTION

Our attitude to money mirrors some of our deepest personal anxieties. I know that there is a streak of meanness in me which is not nice, especially when contrasted with my wife's natural generosity. Giving by standing order is a useful way for me not to slide out of my responsibilities. Always remembering C S Lewis; bracing comment, that giving ten per cent of our income is just the minimum.

SUGGESTION

A useful exercise is for us to write down what our income and regular expenditure is, and how much we give regularly and to whom. And then say to God, "Well, Father, this is me and my money. What now?"

TUESDAY OF LENT 3 - IT WILL BE DESTROYED

*A*s Jesus came out of the temple, one of his disciples said to him, 'Look, Teacher, what large stones and what large buildings!' Then Jesus asked him, 'Do you see these great buildings? Not one stone will be left here upon another; all will be thrown down.'

(Mark 13.1-2)

THE SCENE

The sun was casting long shadows across the Outer Court, the tall Holy Place of the Temple dark against the light of the setting sun.

"Look, Rabbi, at these huge stones! How on earth did they get them here? And these magnificent buildings - they're incredibly beautiful. It must be the finest temple in the world!"

Yeshua stopped dead and turned round to his excited trainees.

"Is that all you see? Big stones? Magnificent expensive buildings? I tell you solemnly, the time is coming when there will be not one stone left upon another. It will all be demolished."

The trainees looked at him aghast - all apart from Y'hudah who had an expression of "I told you so" on his face. Yeshua looked each one in the face. Then, with a shrug, turned round and led the way down to the Kidron.

COMMENT

1 I definitely think that Mark wrote this passage before the Jewish rebellion in 66 AD, and most Biblical scholars think the same. In other words, this was written when the temple was still in full swing, with elaborate daily services using choirs and trumpets, with Temple aristocrats still in charge, supported by a bevy of priests, where three times a year thousands of pilgrims came from all over the Mediterranean to gather for a fortnight of celebration on the hills around Jerusalem. The sun still shone on the golden parapet at the top of the temple, dazzling the eyes of those who approached at dawn from the Mount of Olives. As the rabbis at the time said, "Whoever who has not seen the temple in Jerusalem has not seen a beautiful building." When Mark wrote this, its disappearance must have seemed inconceivable.

And yet a few short years later it was all over. The temple aristocrats had been killed by the revolutionary Jews, who had in turn been killed by the Romans. The city had been set on fire, the temple plundered and the sacred vessels taken to Rome in triumph. Roman soldiers with crowbars had levered the gigantic limestone blocks of the temple walls to crash in splinters on the pavement below. *"All will be thrown down."*

2 Were Jesus' words a prophecy or something else?
There were certainly prophecies of the forthcoming destruction made by the rabbis.

'Forty years before the destruction of the temple... the doors of the sanctuary opened by themselves, until Rabban Yohanan ben Zakkai rebuked them saying, "Oh Temple, Temple! Why do you yourself give the alarm? I know about you that you will be destroyed..."'
(quoted by Neusner 'Life of Yohanan ben Zakkai, p.39)

However, what we have in Jesus' words seems to be a case of prevision, an actual seeing something that is yet in the future. A striking example of this came in the parish magazine of All Saints Hackbridge in 1937. Two workers at

Mullards, the nearby electronics factory, saw and heard, while preparing radios for delivery, a terrifying ghostly apparition of an old woman being burnt to death. Doing some research they found that this had indeed happened at that spot three hundred years before to an old woman called Mother Chisley, who gained the reputation of being a witch and a soothsayer. Her most unbelievable prediction had been of *"strange instruments and devices"* from which would come forth *"musick and ofttimes voices speaking and singing"*. The sounds, she declared, would issue from *"the magical funnel-shaped device within the cabinet"*. Of course, people laughed at her. But it is a remarkable instance of prevision. My guess is that in some way Jesus saw the coming destruction. But like all such spiritual gifts this is more of a curse than a blessing. You see the future but can do nothing to prevent it.

REFLECTION

What happened as a result of the Jewish revolt of 66 CE was to overturn an entire way of life. Just as Covid 19 did for us. Who could have predicted the end of international travel, empty roads, people locked into their own homes all over the world? Yet it happened. We are coming out of it now, but still not sure what the new world order will look like. (This is written in October 2021).

Various reactions are inevitable:

Grief - over what has been lost.

Anger - against those who created the disaster or made it worse.

Nostalgia - that it will all go back to what it was like before.

Hope - that humans will co-operate in creating a better future.

Despair - that the natural self-centredness of human beings will result in greater inequality and suffering, particularly for the most vulnerable.

Doubt - where was God that he should have allowed it to happen?

Faith - that God can create something new out of the ruins of the old.

Sometimes the most faith-filled response is to lament before God. Most of the Psalms are songs of lament. It is as we turn honestly to God with all our pain and doubt that we may find light in our darkness.

SUGGESTION

Write down what has been good and what has been bad about the last few years. Talk to God about it. The Book of Job or Psalms 80 - 88 are good places to start.

WEDNESDAY OF LENT 3 – THE COMING TRIBULATION

When he was sitting on the Mount of Olives opposite the temple, Peter, James, John, and Andrew asked him privately, 'Tell us, when will this be, and what will be the sign that all these things are about to be accomplished?'

Then Jesus began to say to them, 'Beware that no one leads you astray. Many will come in my name and say, "I am he!" and they will lead many astray. When you hear of wars and rumours of wars, do not be alarmed; this must take place, but the end is still to come. For nation will rise against nation, and kingdom against kingdom; there will be earthquakes in various places; there will be famines. This is but the beginning of the birth pangs.

'As for yourselves, beware; for they will hand you over to councils; and you will be beaten in synagogues; and you will stand before governors and kings because of me, as a testimony to them. When they bring you to trial and hand you over, do not worry beforehand about what you are to say; but say whatever is given you at that time, for it is not you who speak, but the Holy Spirit.

'Brother will betray brother to death, and a father his child, and children will rise against parents and have them put to death; and you will be hated by all because of my name. But the one who endures to the end will be saved.

'But when you see the desolating sacrilege set up where it ought not to be (let the reader understand), then those in Judea must flee to the mountains; someone on the housetop must not go down or enter the house to take anything away; someone in the field must not turn back to get a coat. Woe to those who are pregnant and to those who are nursing infants in those days! Pray that it may not be in winter. For in those days there will be suffering, such as has not been from the beginning of the creation that God created until now, no, and never will be. And if the Lord had not cut short

those days, no one would be saved; but for the sake of the elect, whom he chose, he has cut short those days.

'And if anyone says to you at that time, "Look! Here is the Messiah!" or "Look! There he is!"—do not believe it. False messiahs and false prophets will appear and produce signs and omens, to lead astray, if possible, the elect. But be alert; I have already told you everything.

(Mark 13. 1-9, 10-22)

THE SCENE

Yeshua did not speak again as he led the group up the steep path to a cave near the top of the Mount of Olives[1]. He sat down, facing the translucent glow of the Temple in the dusk. One of the trainees used a flint and firesteel to set light to dry tinder, filled an oil lamp from a leather bottle and when the wick was alight, set down the lamp in the middle. The anxious faces of the trainees were now clearly visible, against a backdrop of deep shadows. Two sets of brothers sat near Yeshua, Shim'on Kepha and Andreas, Ya'akov and Yochanan Bar-Zavdai.

"Rabbi, tell us, when will this happen? What will be the signal that all these things are about to take place?"

Yeshua looked at each of them directly. They shifted uncomfortably. Yeshua called the rest of the twelve.

"Come nearer," he said. After the other eight had shuffled closer, he said,

"Watch out! Don't let anyone fool you! Many will come in my name, saying 'I'm the one!' And they will fool many people. When you hear the noise of wars nearby and the news of wars far off, don't become frightened. Such things

133

must happen, but the end is yet to come. For people will fight each other, and nations will fight each other, there will be earthquakes in various places, there will be famines. This is but the beginning of the birth pains.

COMMENT

1 The site

The apocryphal Acts of John, which may date back to the 2nd century, tells us that Jesus used to teach his disciples in a cave on the Mount of Olives. As soon as the Christian faith became legal, a church was built over a cave on the Mount of Olives, called first the Church of the Disciples, soon changed to the Church of the Olive Grove. It was destroyed in.the Persian invasion of 614. During those three hundred years, part of the celebrations of Holy Week was to hold a service there on Tuesday evening and recount Jesus' prophecies of the coming suffering. The crusaders built a church there but after the Muslim conquest it was abandoned and fell into ruins. Five hundred years later Princess Aurelis Bossi acquired the land and built a cloister and a convent. In 1910 the foundations of the Byzantine church were discovered, together with the grotto where by tradition Jesus taught his disciples. The church is now called the Church of Pater Noster as it displays over a hundred different translations of the Lord's Prayer on painted tiles. It is the most tranquil spot in Jerusalem. Do go if you get a chance, even though you have to pay a few shekels and it closes during lunch.

2 The whole of chapter 13 of Mark falls into two sections. First, the coming suffering and the persecution of Jesus' disciples in verses 1 to 22; then the coming of the Son of Man and the end times in verses 23 to 36. Today we look at the first part.

3 What did Jesus say?

Mark 13, and its duplicates in Matthew and Luke, are clearly made up of a series of sayings, not all of which would have been said at the same time. Some of the passages may be made up of later sayings. Verse 10 certainly is a later insertion. But the tradition is firmly embedded in a specific time and space, the Mount of Olives in the last week of Jesus' life.

4 War and famine (v.5-8)

Jesus' four closest friends ask him when his prophecy of the Temple's destruction will take place. Jesus gives an answer that is no answer, simply that wars, and famines will take place, and that these are not to faze them. Indeed, he implies that things will get much worse. And they are not to follow new powerful charismatic prophets who claim to be him.

All this of course could be taken straight out of today's news.

5 Persecution. (v.9-13)

The witnesses to Jesus will be hauled up before councils, kings and governors. This could refer just to the situation in Palestine. Peter and John were taken before the Sanhedrin; James Bar-Zebedee was killed by King Herod Agrippa I; Paul was held in prison for over two years by the Roman governor. The promise is that the Holy Spirit of God will speak through them to those in authority, i.e. continuing Jesus' own calling.

There will also be bitter hostility within their own community and family, *"Brother will betray brother to death".* Just a few years after Jesus' death and resurrection, *'Saul was ravaging the community by entering house after house, dragging out both men and women and committing them to prison.'* (Acts 8.3)

'The one who endures to the end will be saved.' Perhaps 'delivered' would be a better translation. I think it means being delivered from their painful situation, rather than an eternal salvation which is how the later church came to understand it. Of course the whole passage was read differently after the persecution by the emperor Nero in 65, after which it was a capital offence even to be a Christian for the next 250 years.

In the middle of the passage, interrupting the promise of support of the Holy Spirit when on trial, comes the stand-alone sentence: *'And the good news must first be proclaimed to all nations.'* (Mark 13.10). This is surely a later insertion. An early copyist may well have added this comment in the margins of his copy, or between two lines, and it then got included in the main text. Unfortunately it is the one verse that evangelical preachers like to major on in order to make a stirring call to support missionaries. It is not from Jesus.

6 The Desolating Sacrilege (v.14-20)
This passage seems to me to be based on Jesus' pre-vision of the fall of Jerusalem. Things are not in quite the right order. The temple was not desecrated until the end of the siege, whereas the Christian community, warned by Jesus' words, escaped to Pella across the Jordan at the start of the siege. And it certainly was a time of terrible suffering.

7 False Messiahs (v.21-23)
When people live in apocalyptic times, there are always those who make apocalyptic claims. And sometimes it is almost a requirement for the faithful to believe them. Jesus tells us to hold steady, and not invent scenarios in which we think God is about to change things. Jesus' warnings are a call to endure. A Sri Lankan theologian, D T Niles, wrote a commentary about the book of Revelation, called 'Seeing the Invisible', in which he says *"I got to know the Book of*

Revelation during the darkest day of World War II, and it has been my constant companion ever since."

REFLECTION

We all like happy endings. When Prokofiev, the noted Russian composer, wrote his world-famous ballet 'Romeo and Juliet', he started off with giving it a happy ending. It took the whole weight of the Soviet musical establishment to make him turn back to Shakespeare's original tragic conclusion.

Jesus' words in Mark 13 are hard for us to hear, because there is no happy ending. We are not to run after the latest panacea. There is simply the call to endure.

And that is true to life. All of us may well be required to endure even when there will be no happy outcome; either if a loved one is afflicted with dementia, or with a long-standing illness, or when we suffer the effects of global climate change.

Our consolation comes from knowing that we have a companion in our endurance, Yeshua the Son of Man.

SUGGESTION

Read the first three chapters of the Book of Revelation. They give a powerful image of Christ in glory, and of the call on us to obedient faith.

THURSDAY OF LENT 3 - THE COMING OF THE SON OF MAN

*But in those days, after that suffering,
the sun will be darkened,
  and the moon will not give its light,
and the stars will be falling from heaven,
  and the powers in the heavens will be shaken.*

Then they will see "the Son of Man coming in clouds" with great power and glory. Then he will send out the angels, and gather his elect from the four winds, from the ends of the earth to the ends of heaven.

'From the fig tree learn its lesson: as soon as its branch becomes tender and puts forth its leaves, you know that summer is near. So also, when you see these things taking place, you know that he is near, at the very gates. Truly I tell you, this generation will not pass away until all these things have taken place.

Heaven and earth will pass away, but my words will not pass away.

'But about that day or hour no one knows, neither the angels in heaven, nor the Son, but only the Father.

Beware, keep alert; for you do not know when the time will come. It is like a man going on a journey, when he leaves home and puts his slaves in charge, each with his work, and commands the doorkeeper to be on the watch. Therefore, keep awake—for you do not know when the master of the house will come, in the evening, or at midnight, or at cockcrow, or at dawn, or else he may find you asleep when he comes suddenly. And what I say to you I say to all: Keep awake.'

(Mark 13.24-37)

THE SCENE

We frankly do not know when these words were spoken, or when. They seem to have been collected in order to bring several of Jesus' words about the future together in one place, much as Matthew did in the 'sermon on the mount'. What is indisputable is that Jesus said these things or something very like them.

COMMENT

Confession time! When I wrote 'Jesus the Troublemaker' I ignored this passage, which is why it is quoted in full above. My leaving it out is understandable because it is not securely fixed in a specific time and place. But I was wrong to ignore these words, simply because it was through speaking words like these that Jesus got condemned to death by the Sanhedrin.

I will split the passage into three parts, taking them in reverse order.

1 *'Keep awake!'* (vv.33-37)

This is one of the main themes of Jesus' words to his disciples. When speaking to those who did not follow him, his message was different. It was 'Wake up!' It was still the theme of the early church over twenty years later. Paul writing to Christians in Rome says, *"You know what time it is, how it is now the moment for you to wake from sleep. For salvation is nearer to us now than when we became believers; the night is far gone, the day is near. Let us then lay aside the works of darkness and put on the armour of light; let us live honourably as in the day."* (Romans 13.11-13). The message is the same - keep alert, for the final Day of the Lord is coming soon.

Almost two thousand years have passed since then, so it is unrealistic for us to have the same sense of urgency that Jesus and Paul had. But the message for us to have a lifestyle which will gain God's approval is not time-limited.

2 This generation

vv.28-32   All these things will happen in this generation.
Everything will disappear but not my words.
No one at all knows when all these things
will happen.

Here are three contradictory sayings of Jesus about what we should expect when. It is clear that they were not all uttered at the same time in the same breath. They are individual responses of Jesus to questions or attitudes among his hearers which we cannot now retrieve. Rather than focus on the one I feel comfortable with and ignoring the others, I will leave them all to one side.

3 Coming in the clouds

Then they will see the Son of Man coming in the clouds. (vv. 24-27)

I am sorry to say that here is another instance of a tendentious translation. The NRSV puts the words "the Son of Man coming in clouds" in inverted commas, as if to say, this is a quotation and poetry and so does not need to be taken seriously. The NIV thankfully does not make a similar editorial insertion. Since quotation marks were not invented till about 1500, we can ignore the NRSV's use of them.

We do have to take these words seriously. They are what got Jesus crucified.

The high priest asked him, 'Are you the Messiah, the Son of the Blessed One?' Jesus said, 'I am; and you will see the Son of Man

*seated at the right hand of the Power
and coming with the clouds of heaven.'
Then the high priest tore his clothes and said, 'Why do we still
need witnesses? You have heard his blasphemy!*

(Mark 14.61-64 - I have removed the quotation marks)

All the above is quite clear. The only problem is that it has
not happened. So was Jesus misguided?

4 The Cosmic Order

William Barclay's Daily Study Bible on Mark quotes a
number of Jewish writings around the time of Jesus which
use very similar language to Mark 13. For example:

*'The horns of the sun shall be broken and shall be turned
into darkness,
And the moon shall not give her light, and be turned wholly
into blood,
And the circle of the stars shall be disturbed.'*

(The Assumption of Moses 10.5)

Barclay goes on to say, *"In (Mark 13) the one thing we must
retain is the fact that Jesus did foretell that he would come again.
The imagery we can disregard.' (p.335)*

I disagree. As Marshall McLuhan said, *'The medium is the
message.'* The imagery is the language which Jesus and
his fellow Jews used and understood. It is fully a part of
the message.

I remembering reading of missionaries to a tribe in
Tanganyika who translated the Bible into the native
language. They were unsure whether or not to translate
the Book of Revelation in case the Africans could not
understand it. However, they did translate it, and the
tribesmen responded by saying, *"Ah, this we can understand!"*

They understood pictorial language in the way that the left-brained westerners didn't.

The imagery of the sun and moon failing is an image of the whole cosmic order being turned upside down, and instead of being friendly to human life, becoming our adversary. With the crisis of climate change facing humanity, that is not hard to envisage, especially as it is largely caused by human sin/self-centredness.

5 The Cloud

When Jesus said they will see the Son of Man coming in the clouds, he was not predicting the internet! Though the idea that the i-cloud is something without limits or boundaries is a useful analogy.

The cloud is frequently used in the Bible to describe God's palpable presence.

The Lord went in front of them in a pillar of cloud by day, to lead them along the way.

(Exodus 13.22)

The priests could not stand to minister because of the cloud; for the glory of the Lord filled the house of the Lord.

(1 Kings 8.11)

I dwelt in the highest heavens,
and my throne was in a pillar of cloud.

(Ecclesiasticus/Sirach 24.4)

In the New Testament we have the transfiguration, when *'a cloud overshadowed them, and from the cloud there came a voice, 'This is my Son, the Beloved; listen to him!'* (Mark 9.7). And Jesus' ascension six weeks after his death and resurrection, when, *'as they were watching, Jesus was lifted up, and a cloud took him out of their sight.* (Acts 1.9)

Cloud was a sign of the palpable presence of God. It was also a mode of transport between earth and heaven, either down or up. When Jesus spoke of the Son of Man coming in the clouds of heaven, he was talking of the activity of God, not of meteorology. Perhaps a cloud is just what some people experience, as if the effect of the Infinite interacting with the finite is to make things blurry.

REFLECTION

This is That
Perhaps Simon Peter's speech on the day of Pentecost (Acts 2) gives us a clue. The disciples were all inside together in a large room when they experienced a rushing wind, mysterious fire on their heads and being filled with unquenchable praise. They burst out of the house, shouting out God's praise in all sorts of different languages they didn't in fact know. A crowd gathered, some were impressed, some thought they had had too much to drink. Simon Peter stood up and explained:

"These are not drunk, as you suppose, for it is only nine o'clock in the morning.
No, this is what was spoken through the prophet Joel:
In the last days it will be, God declares,
that I will pour out my Spirit upon all flesh,
and your sons and your daughters shall prophesy,
and your young men shall see visions,
and your old men shall dream dreams.
Even upon my slaves, both men and women,
in those days I will pour out my Spirit;
and they shall prophesy.

And I will show portents in the heaven above
  and signs on the earth below,
    blood, and fire, and smoky mist.
The sun shall be turned to darkness
  and the moon to blood,
    before the coming of the Lord's great and glorious day.
    Then everyone who calls on the name of the Lord shall be saved."

(Acts 2.15-21)

I like the 1611 translation of Acts 2.16: *'This is that which was spoken by the prophet...'*

'This is that'. We are not speaking of a one-to-one correlation. Visions or dreams are not part of the story - nor are prophecies in the conventional sense. There was no blood or smoky mist and only a very strange kind of fire. The sun continued in its ordinary course. On the other hand, Joel does not mention talking in other languages. Yet 'this is that'. This is the action of God played out on the human stage.

Son of Man

Many books have been written about what Jesus meant when he spoke of the Son of Man. Did he mean 'I', or mankind in general, or one particular man, or the visionary figure in Daniel 7.13? One thing is clear, that the Son of Man is not God. But you can't separate him from God. The nearest I can think is that he is God's ambassador. So it is pretty important for us to listen to him.

Over to you

This is as far as I can go. It is up to you to make your own conclusions.

SUGGESTION

In Ezekiel 1 the prophet gives a detailed account of his vision of the Lord in glory. He then says, *'This was the appearance of the likeness of the glory of the Lord.'* (1.28)

Make a drawing of the glory of God. Or write some music expressing it. It's impossible, but no more inadequate than words are.

FRIDAY OF LENT 3 – PREPARING THE PASSOVER

*O*n the first day of Unleavened Bread, when the Passover lamb *is sacrificed, his disciples said to him, 'Where do you want us to go and make the preparations for you to eat the Passover?' So he sent two of his disciples, saying to them, 'Go into the city, and a man carrying a jar of water will meet you; follow him, and wherever he enters, say to the owner of the house, "The Teacher asks, Where is my guest room where I may eat the Passover with my disciples?" He will show you a large room upstairs, furnished and ready. Make preparations for us there.'*

(Mark 14.12-15)

THE SCENE

In Beit-Anyah, Yeshua and his trainees had breakfast of barley biscuits dipped in wine, the last time they would have regular bread for the next eight days. Then they went to the local mikvah or ritual bath house and bathed in preparation for Pesach. Outside the mikvah, he gathered his trainees round and spoke to them.

"Today is a great day," he told them, *"We're going to celebrate Aalah's great deliverance of our people, not just then but now. So we are going to eat Pesach in Yerushalayim itself. I'll need two of you to go and make all the preparations, the rest will stay with me in the Temple."*

T'oma said, *"But we've got nowhere in the city. And we don't know if the soldiers might not try to get you. We're safe here."*

"No, T'oma, we're going to fulfil the Torah. We are going to eat Pesach within the city. We'll all go to the Temple together, then you two go out through the Royal Porch to the Upper City. Just south of the City Market is one of the major

cisterns. Wait there till you see a man going down to draw water and take it back up to his house."

"A man! That'll be a turn up for the books!"
"Will he be wearing make-up as well?
"He must be a maid of all work!"

The trainees fell about laughing.

Yeshua smiled broadly. *"Yes, well, you won't mistake him, will you? Follow him, and ask at the house he goes into, 'Our teacher asks where is the guest room where he may eat Pesach with his trainees?' You will be shown a large guest room on the first floor, all set out for us. We'll join you at dusk. And the rest of you, if we get separated, and I'm sure we will, we'll meet outside the Royal Porch after the evening prayers."*

COMMENT

1 This scene was one I remember from the Eagle comic's life of St Mark. In particular, the joke "He must be a maid of all work' is a direct lift. I remember the household steward's appalled reaction when the lady of the house told him to carry a water jar. Carrying water - a very heavy job - is women's work all over the world. But as a secret and obvious sign it was brilliant.

2 It also shows how Jesus had a network of Jerusalem disciples about whom the Galilean Twelve knew nothing. I assume that one of them was Mary, the mother of John Mark, whose house was a natural meeting place for the first followers of the Way (Acts 12.12). In a scene of pure imagination, I give an example of how Jesus might have made the arrangements. And of how it might have impacted Judas Iscariot:

After praying, Yeshua sat down at the side of the Court, next to the Treasury. After a while, a woman, respectably dressed with embroidery on her cloak and with bracelets on her arms, came up to Yeshua.

"Shalom, Rabbi."
"Shalom, Miryam."
"Could I have a word in private?"
"Surely, we'll go into this side room here. Tell me, how are you doing?"
"I'm fine, sad of course, but I'm fine."
"And your son, Yochanan Marcus?"
"Growing up too fast"
Yeshua chuckled as they disappeared from view.

Y'hudah Bar-Shim'on from K'riot looked after them suspiciously.
"What is he plotting now?" he asked T'oma.
"He's not plotting anything, you idiot," T'oma answered.
Y'hudah looked very uncertain, then seemed to come to a decision. He got up and ambled as unobtrusively as he could to the Hall of Polished Stone*

* The Hall of Polished Stone, or the Hall of Hewn Stone, was where the Sanhedrin met.

3 The time needed to prepare for the Passover is never remarked on. The disciples had checked out the house in the first part of the morning, and everything was ready. Apart presumably for the lamb. This had to be bought from the dealers outside the North Gate, sacrificed, then skinned by a priest, taken back to the courtyard of the house and there roasted over a spit for five hours. A full day's work.

REFLECTION

Jesus had this amazing ability both to be present in the moment and to plan in advance. My wife is a wonderful planner, so things get done really well. I tend to sort things out on the spur of the moment. Which is your preferred way of operation?

SUGGESTION

Thank God for who you are. Thank God for someone who works differently from you.

SATURDAY OF LENT 3 – GREEKS

Now among those who went up to worship at the festival were some Greeks. They came to Philip, who was from Bethsaida in Galilee, and said to him, 'Sir, we wish to see Jesus.' Philip went and told Andrew; then Andrew and Philip went and told Jesus. Jesus answered them, 'The hour has come for the Son of Man to be glorified. Very truly, I tell you, unless a grain of wheat falls into the earth and dies, it remains just a single grain; but if it dies, it bears much fruit.'

(John 12.20-24)

THE SCENE

Yeshua was walking in his accustomed area in Solomon's Portico. Shortly after midday, Andreas and Philippos shouldered their way to him.

"Rabbi," Andreas said, *"Philippos has just told me that he met some Greeks from Antioch. They asked him if he was from Galilee and if he knew the prophet Yeshua. And if so, could he introduce them. He wasn't sure how to reply, because they're not from Y'hudah or the Galil, so he asked me. So, Rabbi, do you want us to bring them here so they can meet you?"*

It was rare for Yeshua to be taken aback, but this time he was. *"Well, well, well,"* he murmured to himself. *"So now it starts. Hellenists or goyim?"* he asked Philippos. *"Goyim, Rabbi. That's what made it strange."*

"Strange indeed, Philippos. We are in a new time. In fact the time has arrived for the son of man to come into his own. Amen amen, I tell you, if you want a seed to grow into a plant, you have to bury it in the ground and let it die. Death is the seed-bed of life. Let it die, and a harvest will come.

So now is a time of grief and hope. Of hope and grief. What shall I say? Father, save me from this hour? No, my whole purpose was to come to this hour." He cried aloud, *"Father, may your holy will be carried out!"*

Strangely, out of the clear blue sky came a loud roll of thunder. The faces of everyone in the crowd, even the line of priests, looked up.

"You're wondering what that thunder portends? I'll tell you! It's the Holy One, blessed be he, telling you that his holy will has been carried out and will be carried out!"

Andreas said, *"So, Rabbi, shall I get these Greeks and bring them here?"*

"No, Andreas, it's time for the evening service. Let's go through the Beautiful Gate and pray. And then on to our Pesach supper."

COMMENT

1 This little incident is only recorded in John. There is no reason to doubt it happened. Gentiles were allowed in the Outer Court of the Temple, though to go inside the Beautiful Gate and enter the Court of Israel was a capital offence.

It does seem to have been actual gentile Greeks. A different word is used for Greek-speaking Jews, viz. Hellenists, see Acts 6.1. The word Judaeans could refer either to Jews in general or to the inhabitants of the southern province of Judaea.

2 The phrase 'Very truly I tell you' is translated in the King James Version as 'Verily verily'. In fact the actual words are 'Amen, amen', Hebrew, not Greek. In his devotional commentary on John, Archbishop William Temple argued that what we have here is an actual phrase that Jesus used habitually. Jesus used it as a statement, a bit like the Bellman in Lewis Carrol's 'Hunting of the Snark', who says, *"What I say three times is true."* The phrase occurs repeatedly in John and is used verbatim in the Orthodox Jewish Bible and in the New Catholic Bible. In the other three gospels , the single 'Amen' is often used. I like the idea that what we have in John is an echo of the actual words of Jesus.

3 The parable of the seed needing to die if it is to live is a direct reference to Jesus' coming death. What follow are three short parable-like sayings, similar to what we find in the first three gospels, but presumably added in here because of similar subject matter. Then comes an echo in advance of Jesus' prayer in Gethsemane:

'Now my soul is troubled. And what should I say—"Father, save me from this hour"? No, it is for this reason that I have come to this hour. Father, glorify your name.' Then a voice came from heaven, 'I have glorified it, and I will glorify it again.'

(John 12.27-28)

REFLECTION

John has a very specific understanding of 'glory'. To us glory speaks of victory, joy and praise. We easily attach it to the idea of resurrection. But in John, 'glory' refers equally to the cross, to suffering, to death. In my book I translate 'May your name be glorified" as 'May your holy will be carried out.' The double-sided nature of this glory was hard for the disciples to take in. It is hard for us to take in. But it is the secret at the heart of the Gospel.

SUGGESTION

Think about your life. Has anything taken place for you that was negative but actually created a space which allowed something new to grow? Go for a walk and talk to God about it.

LENT 4

THE UPPER ROOM & GETHSEMANE

Bread and wine at Passover

SUNDAY OF LENT 4 – FOOT-WASHING

*D*uring supper Jesus, knowing that the Father had given all things into his hands, and that he had come from God and was going to God, got up from the table, took off his outer robe, and tied a towel around himself. Then he poured water into a basin and began to wash the disciples' feet and to wipe them with the towel that was tied around him. He came to Simon Peter, who said to him, 'Lord, are you going to wash my feet?' Jesus answered, 'You do not know now what I am doing, but later you will understand.' Peter said to him, 'You will never wash my feet.' Jesus answered, 'Unless I wash you, you have no share with me.' Simon Peter said to him, 'Lord, not my feet only but also my hands and my head!' Jesus said to him, 'One who has bathed does not need to wash, except for the feet, but is entirely clean. And you are clean, though not all of you.' For he knew who was to betray him; for this reason he said, 'Not all of you are clean.'

After he had washed their feet, had put on his robe, and had returned to the table, he said to them, 'Do you know what I have done to you? You call me Teacher and Lord—and you are right, for that is what I am. So if I, your Lord and Teacher, have washed your feet, you also ought to wash one another's feet.'

(John 13.3-14)

THE SCENE

The streets of the Upper City were busy with people moving between houses and slaves making last-minute preparations. Yeshua and his trainees came to a handsome house in the middle of the Upper City, not far from the High Priest's palace. The smell of roast lamb filled the air as they walked through the courtyard to the steps leading to the main guest room, a large upper room about 12 paces by 8. The tables had been beautifully set out with many oil lamps on stands around the room, as well as lamps on the tables. The tables were in the traditional three-sided arrangement, with Yeshua as the host reclining in the middle of the short table at one side, facing all but one of his trainees. Y'hudah IshK'riot reclined behind him and Yochanan directly in front of him.

At the far corner a debate started between the two Ya'akovs as to who should volunteer to do the hand washing for everyone at table. Suddenly, all voices stopped as Yeshua stood up, took off his cloak, and went to the door. There he tied a linen towel around his waist, poured water from the large water jar into a bowl, and came back to the table. He knelt down at Y'hudah IshK'riot's feet, splashed a handful of water on his feet, and wiped them dry with the towel. Shock and embarrassment were on the faces of all the trainees.

At the end he stood up, put on his cloak and reclined in his place again.

"Do you realise what I have done? You call me Rabban and Maran, and you are correct. I am your teacher and master. So if I, your Rabban and Maran, have washed your feet, you also need to wash each other's feet. I have set you an example. It's for you to follow it through."

COMMENT

1 The Vineyard churches, led early on by John Wimber, are one the best outcomes of the charismatic movement of the 1970's. Unusually for evangelical churches, their theology is based on the gospels of Matthew, Mark, Luke and John. The original church is in Anaheim, Los Angeles. In the middle of their welcome area is a life-size statue of Jesus washing his disciples' feet.

The New Testament Church of God, a Pentecostal Church, used to have the practice of always washing each other's feet at every celebration of Holy Communion.

The Roman Catholic, Anglican and other churches include foot washing at the Communion service on Maundy Thursday evening, the day before Good Friday. (Maundy is a corruption of the Latin 'Mandatum' meaning 'commandment'. - "A new commandment I give to you, that you love one another as I have loved you.")

So the story of Jesus washing his disciples' feet is quite significant.

2 Did it happen? The only clear description of it is in John's gospel. Though there may be a sideways allusion to it in Luke 22.27: *'Who is greater, the one who is at the table or the one who serves? Is it not the one at the table? But I am among you as one who serves.'*

A key part in John's account is played by the disciple whom Jesus loved. If, as I believe, this was a Jerusalem disciple called John, perhaps the supper took place in his house. So he was there as the host, sitting with Jesus and the Twelve from Galilee (Mark 14.17). Or was the meal held in the house of Mary, the mother of John Mark, as I tend to believe, see Acts 12.12. So perhaps John and Mary formed a nucleus of Jesus' followers in Jerusalem. But all this is supposition. What is certain is that this incident has had a powerful effect on Christian devotion over the last two thousand years.

3 In 'Jesus the Troublemaker' I assume that Jesus' action did not come out of the blue, but came as a reaction to another of the constant arguments among the Twelve as to who was or should be top of the tree. I wonder if one of the reasons why it was not included in Mark's gospel was because it quickly became a problem. In Acts 6.1-2 Luke tells of tension over daily food distribution between the Aramaic-speaking and Greek-speaking Jews in the community. The response of the twelve was: *"It is not right that we should neglect the word of God in order to wait at tables."* However justified the decision, it is still a bit embarrassing.

REFLECTION

Nowadays foot washing usually occurs in the context of a church service. However, the two most memorable experiences I have had of it were outside church.

Many years ago I was part of a pilgrimage group, headed up by my friend Sister Hilda Mary, walking from Ham, Richmond to Canterbury. We stayed in church halls with a van bringing our rucksacks from one overnight stay to the next. After a few days some of us were getting blisters and a kind fellow pilgrim would wash our feet. Eventually all of us were removing our boots and socks and getting our feet washed at the end of the day. The cold water was sublime! A marvellous way to give and receive love.

Somewhat earlier in my life I went on a pilgrimage to Israel, organised by the chaplain of Imperial College, including many from my local church of St Jude's Earls Court. Maundy Thursday found us staying in a youth hostel in Jerusalem. That evening we had a very informal communion in one of the six-bedded dormitories we were in. We started by washing each other's feet. One of our number had got quite angry with some of the group, and when it came to the foot washing, she could not bear it and got up and left.

Having one's feet washed can be much more difficult to accept than doing it, as Simon Peter's reaction shows. If Jesus had started at one end of the three- sided table, then the first one to have his feet washed would have been Judas Iscariot. It must have been unbearable for him.

SUGGESTION

Central to the lifestyle of members of Alcoholics Anonymous is the requirement to do service, whether welcoming newcomers, serving coffee, putting away the chairs, handling the meeting, finding speakers etc. It is also giving up these jobs after a year.

Is there some helping activity we can take up for our local church or community?

Is there something we should let go to give someone else a chance to contribute?

MONDAY OF LENT 4 - THE PASSOVER

*T*he Lord said to Moses and Aaron in the land of Egypt: This
month shall mark for you the beginning of months; it shall be
the first month of the year for you. Tell the whole congregation
of Israel that on the tenth of this month they are to take a lamb
for each family, a lamb for each household.... You shall keep it
until the fourteenth day of this month; then the whole assembled
congregation of Israel shall slaughter it at twilight. They shall take
some of the blood and put it on the two doorposts and the lintel of
the houses in which they eat it. They shall eat the lamb that same
night; they shall eat it roasted over the fire with unleavened bread
and bitter herbs. ... This is how you shall eat it: your loins girded,
your sandals on your feet, and your staff in your hand; and you
shall eat it hurriedly. It is the passover of the Lord. For I will pass
through the land of Egypt that night, and I will strike down every
firstborn in the land of Egypt... When I see the blood, I will pass
over you, and no plague shall destroy you when I strike the land
of Egypt.

This day shall be a day of remembrance for you.... Throughout
your generations you shall observe it as a perpetual ordinance.
Seven days you shall eat unleavened bread... On the first day
you shall hold a solemn assembly, and on the seventh day a
solemn assembly; no work shall be done on those days; only what
everyone must eat, that alone may be prepared by you. You shall
observe the festival of unleavened bread, for on this very day I
brought your companies out of the land of Egypt...

Then Moses called all the elders of Israel and said to them, 'Go,
select lambs for your families, and slaughter the passover lamb....
You shall observe this rite as a perpetual ordinance for you and
your children. When you come to the land that the Lord will
give you, as he has promised, you shall keep this observance.
And when your children ask you, "What do you mean by this
observance?" you shall say, "It is the passover sacrifice to the

Lord, for he passed over the houses of the Israelites in Egypt, when he struck down the Egyptians but spared our houses." ' And the people bowed down and worshipped.

(Exodus 12.1-27, edited)

While they were eating, Jesus took a loaf of bread, and after blessing it he broke it, gave it to them, and said, 'Take; this is my body.'

(Mark 14.22)

THE SCENE

A servant appeared bringing several plates piled with slices of roast lamb, together with the matzot - unleavened flatbread - bitter herbs and dishes of vegetables. He placed one of each dish in front of Yeshua for him to give the blessings. Yeshua took one of the large flatbreads and broke it in two while saying, *"Barukh ata Adonai Eloheinu, melekh ha'olam, hamotzi lehem min ha'aretz."* - *Blessed are you Lord our God, king of the universe, who brings forth bread from the earth."* Yeshua took a piece himself, reached back and gave one to Y'hudah. As it was being passed down the line, Yeshua said, *"Take, each of you. This is my body. In the future, do this to remember me."* Anxious whispering filled the room. *"What's he saying? What does he mean? Bread - body? I don't understand."*

Yeshua stretched out his hand in blessing over the lamb, the flatbreads and the bitter herbs, and narrated the explanations.

"This is the Passover sacrifice of the Lord, who passed over the houses of our fathers in Egypt when he smote the Egyptians.

"This is the dough of our ancestors, which did not have enough time to rise before the King of kings, the Holy One, blessed be he, appeared to them and redeemed them.

"These are the bitter herbs to remind us that the Egyptians embittered the lives of our forefathers in Egypt with hard labour.

Yeshua was silent for a while and his eyes filled with tears.

"Amen, amen, I say to you, one of you will betray me."

COMMENT

1 A Passover meal?

Was the Last Supper a Passover meal? In Mark it quite clearly is. John's gospel implies that it was a day too early for it to be Passover. Instead, it seems to have been a solemn community meal., a 'chaburah'. This is what the great scholar of the communion service, Gregory Dix, (The Shape of the Liturgy, 1945) argues. Or did Jesus celebrate the Passover a day early? We do not know, but I like the idea of it being a Passover meal. Therefore I include the three statements set out in the Mishnah (c.200 CE) as being the essential core of the Passover meal. The Passover seder (meaning 'order') developed substantially after the destruction of the Temple in 70 CE, but some elements of what the Mishnah records may date from the time of Jesus.

2 Should Christians celebrate a passover seder?

Orthodox rabbis such as Rabbis Poupko and Sandmel say Christians should not, because it takes the focus off the exodus for Egypt and puts it on to Jesus. Others, like the Reform Rabbi Evan Moffic, encourage Christians to conduct a seder. Certainly Messianic Jews and some other churches do annually celebrate the Passover in the traditional way. Whatever the rights and wrongs, it is certain that Jesus could have celebrated the passover as his final meal with his disciples.

And did the early church celebrate the passover? I think it likely. Luke tells us that the early Jesus community prayed daily in the temple (Acts 2.46) and continued with Jewish religious practices. For instance, when Paul visited Jerusalem around 57 CE, James instructed Paul to undergo ritual purification to scotch rumours that he had become anti-Jewish:

"We have four men who are under a vow. Join these men, go through the rite of purification with them, and pay for the shaving of their heads." ... Then Paul took the men, and the next day, having purified himself, he entered the temple with them, making public the completion of the days of purification when the sacrifice would be made for each of them. (Acts 21.23,24,26)

It is very likely that the Jewish Christian community would have celebrated the Passover in their homes. And that would have continued in Jerusalem up to Bar Kochba's revolt in 132 CE, because up to that time all the bishops of Jerusalem were 'of the circumcision', i.e. Jewish Christians.

3 Jews and Christians

In Christian liturgy, especially in the vigil of readings on the night before the celebration of Easter, a direct parallel is made between the miraculous escape from Egypt and the resurrection of Christ. But the latter clearly overshadows the former. For Jews the Exodus is the defining moment when God created and delivered the community of Israel. Whatever tragedies befell the Jewish people in the course of their history, the Passover is still the affirmation that God will continue to create and deliver the Jewish people.

A lot of work is needed to rediscover the Jewish roots of Christianity. We also need to understand Paul's campaign to create a mixed church of both Jews and Gentiles, and what that meant, even though his vision was later lost.

4 "This is my body"

In Mark the words of Jesus over the bread are simply four words, 'This is my body'. In the other accounts, especially Paul in I Corinthians 11 and in Luke, the words 'Do this in remembrance of me' are recorded. Gregory Dix makes the point that the blessing of the bread to which these words were added are not just part of the Passover celebration. The blessing of the bread was spoken by any Jew who ate anything, probably two or three times a day. So did Jesus expect that this act of memorial would take place whenever one of his community said grace over a meal? Should we try to recover that? Or would taking it out of the church context of Holy Communion devalue it?

5 Hocus Pocus

'Hocus pocus' is a phrase denoting pretend magic. If you call something 'hocus pocus' you mean a fraud is going on. However, it is actually a corruption of the Latin phrase at the heart of the mass or communion, 'Hoc est corpus meus', 'This is my body'. It is what Martin Luther said, banging the table, when debating communion with the extreme reformer Zwingli. Both were against the Roman Catholic doctrine of transubstantiation. This doctrine, developed in the middle ages, was based on the idea that there are two levels of reality, the normal physical reality we experience, and an ideal reality existing at a metaphysical level. For example we know a table can have three, four, six or eight legs or even just one central leg, but there is a metaphysical ideal table which underlies all tables. That is what catholics claim about the bread and wine of communion. Zwingli on the other hand said it is simply an act of remembrance.

Luther banged the table emphasising 'Hoc est corpus meus' and said that both the ideal and the real were present in the bread and wine of communion. The English reformers thought that transubstantiation was less objectionable than Luther's ideas. Archbishop Cranmer who wrote the Book of Common Prayer in 1552 came to believe in a spiritual communion, in which the faith of the believer effected a spiritual change by which we *"spiritually eat the body of our Lord Jesus Christ and drink his blood, then we dwell in Christ and he in us, we are one with Christ and he with us."*

Over the last half century discussions between the major churches have come to a common understanding round the word 'memorial'. The churches have moved away from arguments about physical/metaphysical changes. Instead, a temporal change is understood, so that in communion we stand in the real presence of Christ at the Last Supper. Or something like that.

6 Bread?

In most Catholic and Anglican Church, when we come up for communion we receive a small round 'wafer'. This is actually bread pressed and baked at a very high temperature to keep it from going stale. But it is quite unlike what we eat normally as bread. It is not even like the unleavened bread or 'matzot' that Jews eat during the eight days of the Passover/Unleavened Bread, very like crisp Cornish water biscuits. I personally prefer to have something I can recognise as bread. I remember a story I was told by a Roman Catholic missionary in South India. A priest was teaching a group of people and he held up a chapati. *"What is this?"* he asked. *"BREAD"* was the reply. *"And what is this,"* he asked, holding up a host, (round bread from the mass). *"PAPER!"* they replied.

REFLECTION

In the last century all the churches moved towards giving communion to children before they were confirmed, or some similar adult commitment. An objection often voiced was that children would not understand what was happening. But none of us understand! All of us come with empty hands, receive a piece of bread and eat it. The simplest possible action. And one with the deepest resonance of being fed, nurtured, loved.

SUGGESTION

Do what Jesus did. At the beginning of a meal, take some nice bread, hold a piece in your hands and tear it in half.

As you do it, say the Jewish blessing: *"Blessed are you, O Lord our God, King of the universe, who brings forth bread from the earth."*

Share it with your household and spend a few moments thanking God for the good things you enjoy.

TUESDAY OF LENT 4 – THE TRAITOR

When they had taken their places and were eating, Jesus said, 'Truly I tell you, one of you will betray me, one who is eating with me.' They began to be distressed and to say to him one after another, 'Surely, not I?' He said to them, 'It is one of the twelve, one who is dipping bread into the bowl with me. For the Son of Man goes as it is written of him, but woe to that one by whom the Son of Man is betrayed! It would have been better for that one not to have been born.'

(Mark 14.18-21)

THE SCENE

Yeshua was silent for a while and his eyes filled with tears.

"Amen, amen, I say to you, one of you will betray me."

Shock and incredulity was on the face of all the trainees.

"What? No! That can't be true! We've been really careful, honestly. We've not told anyone where we are. The people love you, Rabbi, you're safe here during the feast, surely." After the first shock, each began to say, *"Rabbi, surely I won't be the one to be that stupid?"*

Yeshua said seriously, *"it's one who is sharing bread with me, one of our table fellowship. Didn't David himself say, 'Even my bosom friend in whom I trusted, who ate of my bread, has lifted the heel against me.'*

Shim'on Kefa nodded at Yochanan and mouthed, *"Ask him who it is."* Yochanan leaned back towards Yeshua and whispered, *"Rabbi, who is it?"* Yeshua whispered

169

back, *"The one I give the bread and charoseth to."*

He took a fragment of bread, dipped it in the mud-like charoseth, a mixture of fruit and nuts, leant back and offered it to Y'hudah, who received it with a muted *"I'm honoured, Rabbi."*

"If you need to do something, Y'hudah. now is the time to do it."

The trainee from Judaea hesitated. Yeshua had turned back and all Y'hudah saw was the back of his head. Gritting his teeth, he got up quickly and disappeared into the night.

COMMENT

1 The coming betrayal

This is the only incident during the Last Supper that is common to both Mark and John. John 13.21-30 has more details, but the two accounts are substantially the same. The main point is that when Jesus said that one of the twelve would betray him, they all assumed that the betrayal would be a stupid mistake, one which would let the authorities know how they could find Jesus when he was on his own and unprotected by his Galilean followers. None of them could imagine that one of them would betray him deliberately.

2 Why did Judas betray Jesus?

Various theories have been put forward, many of them mutually contradictory:

a) Judas wanted to force Jesus to reveal his power.

b) Judas wanted a political revolution and throw the Romans out, but that he had got disappointed by Jesus' pacifist stance. (This assumes the name 'Iscariot' comes from the Latin 'sicarios' or dagger-man. I take it to mean 'man from Kerioth')

c) Judas thought that Jesus had given up on the spiritual path and had chosen to ally himself with the Zealot revolutionaries; (this is Dorothy Sayers' supposition in 'The Man Born to be King', 1943)

d) My theory is that Judas let envy and jealousy take him over. We know that the Twelve were already squabbling among themselves. Judas was the only non-Galilean, coming from the southern town of Kerioth in present day Jordan. From the arrival in Jerusalem on, it was clear that Jesus had a separate network of disciples in the Jerusalem area. The coded message to borrow a colt for the triumphal entry, and the secret sign for preparing the room for the last supper made that clear. Did Judas jump ship because he thought he was about to get pushed? The trouble with jealousy is that once you start to let it eat into you, there is nothing the other person can do to persuade you differently.

3 Why did Jesus let Judas betray him?

This is a hard question. He could easily have avoided the arrest simply by returning to Bethany while Judas was out. Jesus could also have confronted him openly about his treachery, and Judas would have had to remove himself very smartly; we know that the disciples had a couple of daggers with them. So was Jesus in effect engineering his own arrest?

The reason may have been that he wanted to force the Sanhedrin's hand. The chief priests and elders had already decided they would not arrest him during festival because the risk of large-scale riots was too great (Mark 14.1-2). Instead they planned to do it afterwards, secretly. Jesus placing himself inside the city at night with only the Twelve with him was an opportunity too good to be missed. But because of the passover crowds, they couldn't afford to keep him in prison, or to have their hands too obviously stained with his blood. Jesus effectively forced them to have a rushed trial. They either had to accept his authority as God's envoy, or kill him.

There is a similarity between Jesus and the Greek philosopher Socrates. Socrates was put on trial in Athens for corrupting young people by his ideas. The way that Greek trials worked is that the prosecution would demand one penalty and the defendant another one. The prosecutor demanded death. Socrates demanded acquittal and a pension for life. The citizens were confronted with a stark choice, and they chose death.

Jesus did not take away Judas' free choice. The disciple from K'riot could have repented at any time, but he didn't.

4 Judgement

The judgement on Judas is harsh: *"It would have been better for him not to have been born."*

I tried to find another similar condemnation in Mark's gospel but only found one:

'If any of you put a stumbling-block before one of these little ones who believe in me, it would be better for you if a great millstone were hung around your neck and you were thrown into the sea. If your hand causes you to stumble, cut it off; it is better for you to enter life maimed than to have two hands and to go to hell, to the unquenchable fire.'

(Mark 9.42-44)

What Jesus is talking about is the seriousness of spiritual rebellion, not a detailed description of the punishment.

REFLECTION

'Holding on to a resentment is like drinking poison and expecting the other person to fall down dead.' The founders of Alcoholics Anonymous discovered that their worst enemy was resentment: 'With the alcoholic, whose hope is the maintenance and growth of a spiritual experience, this business of resentment is infinitely grave. We found that it was fatal.' Resentment, envy and jealousy are poisons to the spirit, but they usually seem beyond our capacity to alter. Jesus taught us to pray, *"Forgive us our debts as we forgive our debtors."* (Luke 11.4). But how do we do forgive?

SUGGESTION

The founders of AA discovered, with the help of the Oxford Group(s), founded by Frank Buchman in 1921, which later grew into Moral Re-Armament, a procedure which really addressed the issue in four steps:

1 Name the person or event which caused our resentment

2 Identify the action which the person did or failed to do which caused our resentment.

3 Identify how their action (or inaction) affected us: What was injured? Our self-esteem (fear), our security (fear), our personal relationships, or our sex relationships?

Now, how can we deal with this?

4 'We realised that the people who wronged us were perhaps spiritually sick.... When a person offended we said to ourselves, "This is a sick person. How can I be helpful to him/her? God, save me from being angry. Thy will be done."

(Alcoholics Anonymous pp.64-67)

Another useful discipline is to pray for someone we dislike every day for a fortnight. Something simple like, "God, bless x and give them what they need."

May we all walk the way of forgiveness.

WEDNESDAY OF LENT 4 – THE BLOOD OF THE COVENANT

(After supper) Jesus took a cup, and after giving thanks he gave it to them, and all of them drank from it. He said to them, 'This is my blood of the covenant, which is poured out for many. Truly I tell you, I will never again drink of the fruit of the vine until that day when I drink it new in the kingdom of God.' When they had sung the hymn, they went out to the Mount of Olives.

(Mark 14.23-26, with phrase from `Luke 22.20)

THE SCENE

Yeshua visibly relaxed. *"Now my task is done. The will of Aalah has been accomplished, and will be accomplished. Lads, I'm going to be with you only a little longer, and you won't know where to find me. There's just one more order I have to give you. Love one another. I have loved you, trusted you, committed myself to you. You do the same for each other. Do I hear an Amen?"*

Heartfelt 'Amens' went round the room. Yeshua started the final thanksgiving

"Barukh ata Adonai Eloheinu, melekh ha'olam, who feeds the whole world with your goodness, with grace, with loving-kindness and with tender mercy. You give food to all beings, for your loving-kindness endures for ever. Through your great goodness food has never failed us. O may it not fail us for ever, for your great name's sake. Blessed are you, O Lord, who gives food to all.

"We thank you, Adonai Eloheinu, because you gave as a heritage to our fathers a desirable, good and pleasant land, and because you brought us forth, Adonai Eloheinu, from the land of Egypt and delivered us from the house of bondage;

175

as well as for the covenant which you have sealed in our flesh; for your Torah which you have taught us; your statutes which you have made known to us; for the life, grace and loving-kindness which you have bestowed upon us, and for the food with which you constantly feed and sustain us every day, in every season and at every hour.

"*Barukh ata Adonai, for the food and the land.*"

Yeshua now took the final cup of wine, the cup of the blessing, and passed it on round the table. As it went round, he uttered these strange words:

"*This cup of wine is the new covenant, the creation of a new community, sealed in my blood, shed for you.*"

One of the trainees almost choked while drinking when he heard this. They all just sat, staring at their Rabbi. What had he just said? What blood? The blood of the Temple sacrifices? A new covenant? What was all this about?

"*Right lads, get up, we'll sing the Hallel.*" The trainees stood and started singing the four last psalms of the Hallel as they went out of the courtyard into the quiet streets of the city.

COMMENT

1 The account of the Last Supper in Mark has been telescoped to just the words of Jesus over the bread and wine at the beginning and end of the meal. The meal actually consisted of four acts rather like a play:

a) Informal conversation while the disciples ate a series of starters, saying their own grace over them. I guess that it was here that Jesus washed the disciples' feet.

b) The formal meal, in which Jesus said the blessing over each different type of food, and introduced the Passover. This is where he said, 'This is my body' as the bread was passed round. This is also where I put the extract from John when Jesus gave a new commandment to his disciples that they should love one another (John 13.34)

c) The great thanksgiving, the climax of the Passover feast. This is a shortened version of the prayer in 'the Jewish Authorised Daily Prayer', compiled by Rabbi S Singer and used by Dom Gregory Dix in 'The Shape of the Liturgy' p.53.

d) The conclusion: the final cup of wine and singing of the Hallel.

In a Passover seder today four cups are passed round at different points of the meal, each symbolising one of the promises of God in Exodus 6.6-7: 'I will bring you out of the burdens of the Egyptians'; 'I will deliver from bondage'; 'I will redeem you'; 'I will take you as my people and I will be your God'.

We do not know if this practice of four cups of wine was current in Jesus' day. Luke mentions two cups. The final cup 'after supper' (Luke 22.20, 1 Corinthians 11.25) was the occasion of Jesus' words, *"This is my blood of the covenant, poured out for many."* (Mark 14.25)

2 Distasteful?
My father was Jewish (he lived to over a hundred), but very supportive of me as a Christian and a priest. He would come

to church when he stayed with us. One day he confided to me how distasteful he found the communion service. "It sounds like cannibalism," he said. That must have been the immediate reaction of the disciples. What would Jesus have expected them to understand by it? Here they were, meeting in the shadow of the Temple, where literally thousands of lambs had had their throat slit that day, and bowls of their blood thrown against the altar. This is my blood' must have spoken to them of both death and sacrifice.

3 Sacrifice

In her marvellous little book 'Sacrifice and the Death of Christ', the theologian Frances Young tells how in the ancient world sacrifice and worship were almost coterminous. Anything you wanted to do in worship, whether thanksgiving, praise, confession or petition would be framed by an animal sacrifice. In my short time in India I saw a` goat being sacrificed - having her throat slit, as a thank-you for some healing received at the shrine. I also saw a vegetarian sacrifice at the laying of the foundation of a training school for the village. The Christian pastor read a Psalm. The Hindu priest cut a lime in half with something added which turned the lime juice into the exact colour of blood.

So when Jesus implied that his forthcoming death would be a sacrifice, what did he mean by it?

3 Covenant

"This is my blood of the covenant, poured out for many."

What this does not say is that his sacrifice is redemptive - redeeming us from our sins. The idea of redemption is in the Passover seder, but would come earlier in the meal. Nor was it an act of thanksgiving (very obviously). It was a covenant sacrifice - something which would create a new people and a new relationship with God: *'I will take you as my people and I will be your God'* (Exodus 6.7)

The nature of this covenant-making is described in Exodus 24.6-8:

Moses rose early in the morning, and built an altar at the foot of the mountain, and set up twelve pillars, corresponding to the twelve tribes of Israel. He sent young men of the people of Israel, who offered burnt-offerings and sacrificed oxen as offerings of well-being to the Lord. Moses took half of the blood and put it in basins, and half of the blood he dashed against the altar. Then he took the book of the covenant, and read it in the hearing of the people; and they said, 'All that the Lord has spoken we will do, and we will be obedient.' Moses took the blood and dashed it on the people, and said, 'See the blood of the covenant that the Lord has made with you in accordance with all these words.'

We may not like the idea of bowlfuls of blood first being thrown against the altar and then thrown at us, but it was a powerful symbol of the new life-creating bond between God and the people. The way this covenant was expressed in daily life was in obeying 'the book of the covenant' - notably the Ten Commandments of Exodus 20.

Jesus is implying that his death will create another covenant, open to 'the many' - to Jews for whom the former covenant had stopped creating that life-giving bond with God, but also, by implication, to the nations of the world. No boundaries are specified!

4 The imminent kingdom
Amen I tell you, I will never again drink of the fruit of the vine until that day when I drink it new in the kingdom of God.'

(Mark 14.25)

At the end of this solemn Passover meal, Jesus clearly expects his death to usher in the end of human history, in which, to quote Paul, *'the creation itself will be set free from its bondage to decay and will obtain the freedom of the glory of the children of God.'* (Romans 8.21).

It certainly did not feel like that during the despairing sabbath that followed the crucifixion. The following day, Sunday, was quite a turnaround. As Jesus says in John 16:

"Amen amen, I tell you, you will weep and mourn, but the world will rejoice; you will have pain, but your pain will turn into joy. When a woman is in labour, she has pain, because her hour has come. But when her child is born, she no longer remembers the anguish because of the joy of having brought a human being into the world. So you have pain now; but I will see you again, and your hearts will rejoice, and no one will take your joy from you."

(John 16.20-22)

REFLECTION

For me in the Church of England a sad things about the Covid 19 lockdown was the withdrawal of the wine from the people. The priest continued to take it. We were told that by taking the bread we were in fact taking the bread and wine together. It certainly did not feel like that. And it was probably unnecessary. 'Intincting', or dipping the bread into the wine and then eating it was a pretty safe option. A little country church in Bigbury, Devon, thought up an excellent way, taking a leaf from the Baptists and Methodists. We queued up to receive a piece of bread from the vicar, went to a side chapel where a churchwarden gave each of us a small plastic glass of wine and we returned to our seats. The vicar then spoke the words of administration and we all ate the bread and drank the wine together. Why were there not other imaginative solutions sought, instead of relying on a

piece of bloodless pre-reformation theology?
What is special about the wine? I suppose that wine as a
liquid feels a bit nearer to blood, than does a small piece
of bread to flesh. This makes the symbolism feel more
powerful and more personal. Colin Buchanan, bishop
of Woolwich, conducted a long campaign to amend the
Prayer of Humble Access in the Book of Common Prayer
communion service. In it we ask for *'our sinful bodies to be
made clean by his body, and our souls refreshed by his precious
blood'*. Bishop Colin argued that this distinction made
little sense, However, the original words have at last been
retained. They may not be quite accurate theologically, but
they do speak to our ordinary human condition.

SUGGESTION

The hymn which the disciples sang at the end of the feast
were known as the Hallel psalms (so-called because they all
start with the word 'praise'). These were psalms 113 to 118.
Psalms 113 and 114 were said at the start of the meal, the
remaining four at its conclusion.

I suggest you stand up and say aloud Psalm 118. Make a note
of those verses which seem particularly appropriate to this
season of Good Friday and Easter.

THURSDAY OF LENT 4 - THE DESERTERS

Jesus said to them,
'You will all become deserters; for it is written,
"I will strike the shepherd, and the sheep will be scattered."
But after I am raised up, I will go before you to Galilee.'
Peter said to him, 'Even though all become deserters, I will not.'
Jesus said to him, 'Truly I tell you, this day, this very night, before
the cock crows twice, you will deny me three times.'
But he said vehemently, 'Even though I must die with you, I will
not deny you.' And all of them said the same.

(Mark 14.27-31)

THE SCENE

The group walked past Herod's palace and the Roman barracks which doubled as the governor's residence. when he was in Jerusalem, as now. They went through the gate next to the Hippichus Tower and followed the track around the outside of the city wall which would lead them to the Kidron valley.

Almost immediately, Yeshua stopped and stared at the small rocky hill to their left. The full moon shone on it so that the sides gleamed like silver. On top of it half a dozen upright wooden posts stood silhouetted black against the night sky.

"*Skull Hill,*" murmured Yeshua. "*How long, Adonai, how long?*" He turned to the worried trainees. "*I have to make you ready,*" he said. "*You have followed me all the way, through all the difficulties. I now declare to you that you will all sit with me at table when Aalah's kingly rule finally comes. But just for now, you will all desert me.*"

"No, Rabbi, that's impossible - unthinkable!" each one exclaimed.

"Listen! It says in the Law and the Prophets, '"I will strike the shepherd, and the sheep will be scattered.' And no word of the Readings can stay unfulfilled. But take heart! After I have been raised, I will meet you in the Galil."

Shim'on Kefa almost shouted his response. *"NEVER, Rabbi, never will I desert you! Even though everyone else runs away, I won't!*

"Really? Amen, amen, before we hear the second bugle signalling dawn, you will have said three times that you don't know me."

"No. NO! Even if it means dying with you! I'll never do it!"

"That goes for me too!" "And me." "You can rely on me, Rabbi." "I'll never leave you in the lurch!"

Yeshua looked sadly at the group of upset men. Then he focussed on Shim'on Kefa standing in the middle, looking as if he wanted to hit someone hard.

"Oh Shim'on, Shim'on, the Enemy has insisted on putting all of you through the shredder. But I have prayed for you, for you Shim'on, and when you are yourself again, encourage your brothers."

They continued their walk round the walls. When they had left the domineering walls of the Antonia Fortress behind them and were about to descend into the Kidron Valley, just before the steep descent, Yeshua turned to his trainees.

"Tell me, when we were in the Galil, did we have any problems with food and drink and shelter?"

"No, everyone was very welcoming, very generous."

"It's not going to be like that any more. If you've got a wallet, take it. If you've got a rucksack, that's ideal. If you've got a dagger to defend yourself, don't go out without it."

Shim'on Zelotes, proud to be of use for once, said, "I've got one here."

"Me too," said Taddai.

"Enough already!" exclaimed Yeshua. He turned and began the descent, shaking his head.

COMMENT

1 The words of Jesus to his disciples after the Last Supper are recorded plainly, but not their setting. Where they were said depends on the location of the upper room where the feast was held. The key geographical constraint is that Gethsemane was on the opposite side of the Temple from where the Last Supper was held, and the gates were presumably shut after dark. So Jesus had to go to Gethsemane either clockwise round the city walls to the north via the gate by the Hippichus Tower, or anti-clockwise through the Valley or Fountain Gate to the south. My view is that the Syrian Orthodox claim for St Mark's Church to be the site of the upper room is the more persuasive. This would lead to Jesus walking north, right past the rocky hill of Golgotha. Hence the dramatic reconstruction of the scene as described above.

2 The interesting point about Mark's account of Jesus foretelling that Simon Peter would deny him three times, is that this will happen before the cock crows twice. (The other gospels omit this detail). That is very specific, especially as there would be any number of hens and roosters in and around Jerusalem. William Barclay in his Daily Study Bible suggests that the phrase refers to the Latin word 'gallicanium' meaning 'cockcrow'. It was also used for the bugle call which announced the changing of the watch after each quarter of the night hours, 9.00, 12,.00, 3.00, 6.00. This would have been heard all over Jerusalem from both the Antonia fortress and the Roman barracks in part of Herod the Great's palace. Depending on when Jesus said these words, this would mean Peter would deny him either after midnight that night, or more likely, after 3.00 am.

3 *"You will all become deserters."* What a hard thing for the disciples to hear. Not that they are going to put up a fight and lose, but that they will run away. How hard to live with yourself afterwards. It reminds me of the Soviet invasion of Czechoslovakia in 1968, which I came within two weeks of witnessing first-hand. The entire reforming politburo were arrested and taken to Russia, but before doing so they issued an announcement that there was to be no armed resistance at all, not from the army, not from the general population. Otherwise there could have been an absolute bloodbath. Instead there was a week of total civil disobedience which the Russians were not able to counter. They were forced to bring back Dubcek and his government for a time. A remarkable story. Had the disciples been brave and resisted, there would not have been eleven disciples to be greeted by the risen Jesus three days later.

4 Luke records Jesus as saying that from now on, instead of being popular wherever they went, now every man's hand would be turned against them. This might be more than a warning, an instruction for them to be prepared. It may also imply that they will share in the rejection which Jesus himself would suffer. They too would play their part in the tribulation which would ultimately herald the coming of the kingdom of God. There may be a hint of this in Paul's mysterious remark to the Christians at Colossae: *'I am now rejoicing in my sufferings for your sake, and in my flesh I am completing what is lacking in Christ's afflictions for the sake of his body, that is, the church.'* (Colossians 1.24)

5 Of course, these words of warning have comparatively little resonance to us in the comfortable West. But in the rest of the world suffering for the sake of Christ is an ever-present danger. Some examples are the kidnapping, murder and destruction taking place in northern Nigeria, the imminent danger of death in Afghanistan; the mob violence in India, condoned by the extremist Hindu authorities (and suffered by Muslims as well); the imprisonment of Christians in many countries for violating anti-Christian laws. The words of the writer of the Letter to the Hebrews is a reflection of the stark reality of millions of Christians in the world today:

Recall those earlier days when, after you had been enlightened, you endured a hard struggle with sufferings, sometimes being publicly exposed to abuse and persecution, and sometimes being partners with those so treated. For you had compassion for those who were in prison, and you cheerfully accepted the plundering of your possessions, knowing that you yourselves possessed something better and more lasting.

(Hebrews 10.32-34)

REFLECTION

A question which used to be asked of congregations when I was younger was, 'If it was a crime to be a Christian, would there be enough evidence to convict you?' In general I dislike questions designed to make people feel guilty, but this is a pertinent question. A recent booklet was published by Grove Books on 'Seeing ourselves as others see us : Perceptions of the Church of England'. According to research, the Church of England is known for its good works such as food banks. But in terms of faith or prayer or spirituality it is regarded as virtually non-existent.

'My brothers, this ought not to be so!' (James 3.10)

What I turn the spotlight on myself, I find the following:

> I am regular at worship on Sundays and am open about this to anyone.
> I aim to pray in the morning and at night, but keep it private.
> I used to wear a 'Jesus fish' but no longer do so.
> I am happy to talk to people about the books I write about the Bible, but rarely anything more personal.
> I don't at the moment work as a volunteer at a shelter for homeless people or in prison, though I did so before the pandemic.

So, is there enough evidence to convict me, or not?

Ask yourself some similar questions.

SUGGESTION

Spend some time looking up current instances of persecution of Christians. An excellent resource is the Barnabas Fund, which provides very helpful daily pointers for prayer. See barnabasfund.org. There are of course many others. Do some research, and then pray!

FRIDAY OF LENT 4 – GETHSEMANE

They went to a place called Gethsemane; and he said to his disciples, 'Sit here while I pray.' He took with him Peter and James and John, and began to be distressed and agitated. And he said to them, 'I am deeply grieved, even to death; remain here, and keep awake.' And going a little farther, he threw himself on the ground and prayed that, if it were possible, the hour might pass from him. He said, 'Abba, Father, for you all things are possible; remove this cup from me; yet, not what I want, but what you want.' He came and found them sleeping; and he said to Peter, 'Simon, are you asleep? Could you not keep awake one hour? Keep awake and pray that you may not come into the time of trial; the spirit indeed is willing, but the flesh is weak.' And again he went away and prayed, saying the same words. And once more he came and found them sleeping, for their eyes were very heavy; and they did not know what to say to him.

(Mark 14.32-40)

THE SCENE

When they got to Gat Sh'manim, Yeshua went through the gate in the low stone wall, followed by the trainees.

"It's late, why aren't we going straight to Beit Anyah?" grumbled Mattatyahu to Yaakov BenChalfai.

"We've got to wait for Y'hudah. We don't want him being picked up by the police."

Yeshua said to the trainees, *"I know you're tired. Have a break and relax for the time being. Shim'on Kefa, Ya'akov and Yochanan, come with me. I need to pray."*

They walked past the large stone olive press, with the wooden beam for donkeys to turn the giant millstone.

On the other side, Yeshua said, *"Stay here. I'm going on a little further."* He went another fifty paces into the shade of the olive grove and crouched down, his head in his hands. *"Abba, Abba,"* he cried, *"you can do anything. Take away this cup of suffering. Deliver me from my enemies. Oh my help, come quickly to my aid! But...but. Your will, Abba. Your will be done. Your will be done."* He slowly got up and walked back through the orchard. The night was completely silent apart from the coo-ick of a distant nightjar. All three trainees were asleep, and no sound came from the other group. Yeshua, shook them awake. *"Come on, my brothers, try to stay awake. I want you to be with me tonight. It's hard for me."*

He went back to the former spot and prayed in the same way, but when he returned they were out like a light again. Once more he woke them up, but the third time he let them sleep.

COMMENT

1 Gethsemane

I always assumed that 'Gethsemane', in Hebrew Gat Sh'manim, meant something like 'olive grove'. In fact it means olive press - the enormous millstone pulled round and round by a donkey to crush the olives to a paste, then the long process of pressing the paste in order to release the oil. So 'Gethsemane' was actually a large stone building, set within a garden of olive trees (John 18.1). Archaeologists have recently found a 1st century 'mikvah' or ritual bath house by it, presumably for the workers in the olive press, so that the oil produced would be ritually pure and could be sold to the Temple.

2 Meeting place

The gospel of John tells us that Judas Iscariot knew the place because Jesus often meet there with his disciples (John 18.2). The irony is that the eleven disciples knew they were there to wait for Judas to come out from the city and go back to Bethany together. Jesus knew he was waiting there to be captured by his enemies, led by Judas. He deliberately did not change his normal practice.

3 Abba

'Abba' was how Jesus talked to God, his actual word. Abba was the intimate, family word for father in Aramaic, Jesus' home language. Jesus had this understanding of God from his earliest days. When he was twelve years old he got lost in Jerusalem for three days. When his anxious parents found him , he said, *"Why were you searching for me? Didn't you know that I must be in my Father's house?"* (Luke 2.49) 'Abba' expressed Jesus' total trust and reliance on God. Now it was put to the ultimate test.

4 Agony

Jesus told his three closest friends, *"I am deeply grieved, even to death."* His agonised prayer was for God to *"remove this cup from me."* In Luke's account his prayer was so intense that *'his sweat was like great drops of blood falling onto the ground.'* (Luke 22.44). (Note - it does not say he actually sweated blood - that's a product of later Christian imagination).

What caused Jesus' agony?

He had already foreseen his painful death - that would have been enough for most.

There was the uncertainty. Would he be condemned to death or might something else happen - prison, exile, whipping, stoning?

There was his climactic confrontation with Jewish authorities. Would he truly be God's witness to Israel's leaders?

From being a man of honour in the eyes of the people, how could he bear to become a figure of shame because of his obedience to God?

There certainly was enough for Jesus to cry out, "Remove this cup from me!"

5 Your will be done

Throughout his life Jesus had been centred on doing God's will. The Lord's Prayer in Matthew 6.10. parallels 'your will be done' with Jesus' signature message, 'your kingdom come.' The gospel of John emphasises over and over again the completely alignment of Jesus' will with that of his Father: *"I do as the Father has commanded me, so that the world may know that I love the Father."* (John 14.31)

Now Jesus makes the final handing over of his life and mission to his Father: *'Not what I want, but what you want'*. He had to have three separate times of prayer in order to embed his surrender into his very being. At last that work was done and he came to a place of peace.

'Are you still sleeping and taking your rest? Enough! The hour has come; the Son of Man is betrayed into the hands of sinners.'
(Mark 14.41)

6 The foundation stone of the Christian life

Who or what runs my life? Often it is fear of some sort - fear of failure, fear of pain, fear of others, fear of authority, fear of unpopularity, fear of emptiness, fear of missing out. Surrendering our lives to God trumps all other fears. If the idea of surrendering our lives to God doesn't scare us, it's not real. But if we do manage it, for instance by kneeling down and saying to God, "Over to you", we will receive an inner freedom which is unequalled. But the process is not easy. Susan Howatch the novelist described it as like being 'slammed up against a wall until my teeth rattled'.

SUGGESTION

A prayer to think about. Methodist churches hold an annual Covenant Service in which members rededicate their lives to God. Here is the Covenant Prayer:

> I am no longer my own, but thine.
> Put me to what thou wilt, rank me with whom thou wilt.
> Put me to doing, put me to suffering (or rather, patient endurance).
> Let me be employed for thee or laid aside for thee, exalted for thee or brought low for thee.
> Let me be full, let me be empty.
> Let me have all things, let me have nothing.
> I freely and heartily yield all things to thy pleasure and disposal.
> And now, O glorious and blessed God, Father, Son and Holy Spirit, thou art mine, and I am thine.
> So be it.
> And the covenant which I have made on earth, let it be ratified in heaven.
> Amen.

Or more simply, 'Your will, not mine, be done.'

SATURDAY OF LENT 4 - ARREST

Jesus came a third time and said to them, 'Are you still sleeping and taking your rest? Enough! The hour has come; the Son of Man is betrayed into the hands of sinners. Get up, let us be going. See, my betrayer is at hand.'

Immediately, while he was still speaking, Judas, one of the twelve, arrived; and with him there was a crowd with swords and clubs, from the chief priests, the scribes, and the elders. Now the betrayer had given them a sign, saying, 'The one I will kiss is the man; arrest him and lead him away under guard.' So when he came, he went up to him at once and said, 'Rabbi!' and kissed him. Then they laid hands on him and arrested him. But one of those who stood near drew his sword and struck the slave of the high priest, cutting off his ear. Then Jesus said to them, 'Have you come out with swords and clubs to arrest me as though I were a bandit? Day after day I was with you in the temple teaching, and you did not arrest me. But let the scriptures be fulfilled.' All of them deserted him and fled.

A certain young man was following him, wearing nothing but a linen cloth. They caught hold of him, but he left the linen cloth and ran off naked.

(Mark 14.41-51)

THE SCENE

Suddenly there was a noise at the entrance gate of the olive grove.

Jesus spoke urgently. *"Quickly! Wake up! The traitor is here!"*

The three trainees stood up groggily. There was a confused noise as the other trainees woke up and realised that they were confronted by a posse of Temple guards and Roman soldiers. They scattered among the olive trees, but stopped when they realised they were not being pursued. They realised that the one leading the armed mob with their lanterns and flaming torches was their friend Y'hudah. They were completely confused.

Yeshua strode forward past the olive press into the light of the lanterns.

"Are you looking for someone?" he asked the group of men armed with truncheons and swords. Their self-confidence was shaken and there was a pregnant pause. Then Y'hudah came forward, kissed Yeshua on the cheek and said, *"Shalom, Rabbi".*

"My friend, do you betray the son of man with a kiss?" asked Yeshua quietly. As if on a signal, the armed crowd surged forwards and two of them grabbed Yeshua by the arm. Shim'on Zelotes shouted *"NO!"*, pulled out his dagger and slashed at the head of one of the men holding Yeshua. The man moved to get out of the way and then screamed as his ear was almost severed.

"STOP IT!" shouted Yeshua and there was a stunned silence. Yeshua held the injured man's head in both hands for a moment. The man stood there dazed, then staggered back, touching this ear, not quite believing that the bleeding had stopped.

Yeshua took a deep breath, then spoke strongly.

"Are you really coming to get me in the middle of the night with billy clubs and swords? Do you really think I'm a dangerous bandit? Every single day this week I have been in the Temple teaching, praying, talking. No one laid a finger

on me then. But I guess that darkness suits you. Only, let these men go."

The Roman decurion shouted, *"Arrest him!"* The group of Romans soldiers and Temple guards ran forward and grabbed him, and some started after the trainees who scattered in fear. One young man was spotted because the white sheet he had wrapped himself in gave him away, but he wriggled out of it and ran off naked. The centurion shouted again, *"Come back, men, we've got the guy we want."* The soldiers handed Yeshua over to the Temple guards who tied his wrists tight behind his back, and pushed him roughly up the road back to Yerushalyim.

COMMENT

1 Four accounts

Each of the four gospels has a slightly different account of the arrest of Jesus, not surprising in view of the darkness and confusion. The basis of my account is Mark, but I have added details from the other gospels.

I believe John's account when he says that the arresting party was composed of both Roman troops and Temple guards, *'a detachment of soldiers together with police from the chief priests and the Pharisees, and they came there with lanterns and torches and weapons.'* The authorities did not know if they were going to have a fight on their hands so they needed to have serious back-up. This also implies that Caiaphas the high priest must have liaised with Pilate to get the troops, while he also arranged with the governor for a quick rubber-stamping job in the morning to ratify the Sanhedrin's condemnation of Jesus. This was suggested in the book 'Who Moved the Stone?' by Frank Morrison, an idea I find convincing.

John also has Jesus effectively taking charge of his own arrest, with the soldiers falling back in confusion. Again, possible. To arrest a powerful prophet or wonder-worker or magician at midnight would test the nerves of most men of the time.

I take Judas' greeting of Jesus with the customary kiss as the way he broke the spell. It was also a necessary sign to the soldiers, otherwise they would not have known which of the bearded figures was Jesus. There were no photographs then.

2 Violence

There are different accounts of the violence that took place. Mark tells us that one of the eleven used his sword and cut off the ear of the servant of the high priest.

Luke repeats Mark but says that Jesus healed him.

John specifies that it was Simon Peter who attacked the slave, whose name was Malchus.

I find it a problem that Simon Peter is not named in Mark's account. Traditionally Mark acted as interpreter and scribe for Simon Peter on his missionary travels. If it was Peter who struck the blow, I would expect him to be named. So I have guessed that it was a different Simon who lunged forward with his long dagger, Simon the Zealot, who was at least used to the idea of violence.

And what about the healing of Malchus' ear? Is Luke right? Did Jesus heal him? Who knows?

Certainly Jesus put a very quick end to any act of resistance by his disciples. The soldiers ran after them, but they all escaped in the darkness.

3 Mark?

Only Mark has the curious detail of the young man, i.e. a teenager, there with only a sheet wrapped around him. The soldiers tried to grab him, but only got hold of the sheet. He wriggled out of it and ran off.

Who was he? The only sensible guess is that it was the person writing the gospel. He put it in, because he was there. How did he come to be there? My guess is taken from the life of St Mark published by the Eagle comic when I was a schoolboy. The story as drawn was that Mark went to sleep on the roof when Jesus left his mother's house after the Last Supper. He was wakened by Judas arriving with the Roman and Temple guards. He nipped downstairs and rushed to try to get a warning to Jesus, but arrived only just in time to witness the arrest.

4 Christian pacifism

Jesus' attitude is clear. You do not fight God's battles with guns - or anything else. Sometimes the Church has used its position in society to attack those with whom it disagrees. The Church of England today is a relatively safe church to belong to because it has almost no power. When it did possess power, as in the16th and 17th centuries, Roman Catholics, Puritans and Quakers sometimes suffered severely. John Bunyan's 'Pilgrim's Progress' was written partly in Bedford prison where he had been put for being an unlicensed preacher. Sometimes the persecuting boot was on the other foot, as in the massacre of thousands of Protestant Huguenots in Paris on St Bartholomew's Day 1572. God must look at the history of the church, indeed of all religions, and say frequently to himself 'not in my name'.

Does this mean that general pacifism is a necessary mark of Christian ethics? Certainly it was in the early church. When candidates for baptism were presented to the bishop of

Rome in the third century, if they were soldiers they would be asked, *"If you are ordered to kill, will you disobey the order?"* If the answer was 'no', they were told to come back later when they were ready to give a different answer.

Could I kill? I think the answer is yes. If I had been in Czechoslovakia during the Warsaw Pact invasion of 1968, and had been asked to shoot any Russian coming over a bridge, I think I would have done it.

5 The Hour of Darkness

Humans are very good at creating darkness: Nazi death camps in which 6 million Jews and 3 million Poles were killed; genocide of the Armenians by Ottoman turks in 1915, of Tsutsis in Rwanda, of Rohingya Muslims in Myanmar; the Chinese and Korean victims of Japanese aggression in the early 20th century, and the Japanese victims of Hiroshima and Nagasaki; oppression of whole nations, classes and genders, as with Palestinians, black Africans under South African apartheid, the Matabele by the Shona in Zimbabwe, the Uighur Muslims in China, women in Afghanistan; the destruction of civil society in Syria etc. etc. The result of all the darkness in the world is that there are more refugees now than at any time in human history; over 82.5 million, including 48 million internally displaced.

The hurried arrest of Jesus by night stands as a token for all the wrongful use of political and mob power.

6 A Christian's response

A young farm boy from the Sudetenland, Germany, wrote this letter to his parents on February 3rd 1944:

"Dear parents: I must give you some bad news - I have been condemned to death, I and Gustave G. We did not sign up for the SS, and so they condemned us to death... Both of us would

*rather die than stain our consciences with such deeds of horror.
I know what the SS has to do.... Many more parents will lose
their children. Many SS men will get killed too. I thank you
for everything you have done for my good since my childhood;
forgive me, pray for me...*

(from 'Dying we Live - final messages of
some Germans who defied Hitler' 1956)

SUGGESTION

TV crime dramas always feature a board full of photographs
in an 'incident room' relating to the crime being
investigated. How about creating your own 'incident board'
or 'incident wall' with pictures of cruel events and their
victims around the world as a focus for your prayers?

An appropriate prayer is the perhaps the most ancient
Christian prayer of all:

'Lord, have mercy.'

LENT 5

ON TRIAL

Praetorium/Governor's headquarters

SUNDAY OF LENT 5 – "I DO NOT KNOW THE MAN"

Peter had followed Jesus at a distance, right into the courtyard of the high priest; and he was sitting with the guards, warming himself at the fire.… One of the servant-girls of the high priest came by. When she saw Peter warming himself, she stared at him and said, 'You also were with Jesus, the man from Nazareth.' But he denied it, saying, 'I do not know or understand what you are talking about.' And he went out into the forecourt. Then the cock crowed. And the servant-girl, on seeing him, began again to say to the bystanders, 'This man is one of them.' But again he denied it. Then after a little while the bystanders again said to Peter, 'Certainly you are one of them; for you are a Galilean.' But he began to curse, and he swore an oath, 'I do not know this man you are talking about.' At that moment the cock crowed for the second time. Then Peter remembered that Jesus had said to him, 'Before the cock crows twice, you will deny me three times.' And he broke down and wept.

(Mark 14.54, 66-72)

THE SCENE

It was now the middle of the night, with the moon high overhead. The posse with their prisoner marched back up the hill, past the Pool of Bethesda, and up to the Antonia Fortress. Here the Roman officer and soldiers left them. The Temple guards took their prisoner through the gate leading to the grand Hasmonean palace. Part of it was the palace of Anan the senior high priest, father-in-law to the official High Priest Kayafa. Yeshua was marched into its courtyard. After a lengthy pause with men running into and out of the palace, Yeshua was taken into the main hall.

(After the investigation by Annas) the guards marched Yeshua through the large courtyard, lit by the flickering flames of a charcoal brazier. Just then the bugle call sounded from the Antonia, marking the start of the late night watch. Yeshua's gaze rested for a moment on the grief-stricken face of Shim'on Kefa standing at the back of the mixed crowd of servants and soldiers, curious about the fate of the northern preacher. Yeshua's face remained impassive as he was hustled out of the front archway into the quiet dark streets of the Upper City.

COMMENT

1 The weather

Nights get cold in Jerusalem. It often snows there in February and this is less than two months later. It was a full moon and I guess that the night was clear. That meant that after sunset the temperature would drop sharply; which is why the servants and soldiers made sure there was a good brazier going in the middle of the courtyard and why Simon Peter got nearer than was wise.

2 Which high priest?

Simon Peter made his denial during the trial of Jesus in front of the high priest. But which one? Mark says it was Caiaphas. John said it was Caiaphas' father-in-law Annas.

The official high priest at the time was Joseph Bar-Caiaphas, appointed by a new Roman prefect in 18 CE. He continued in post until Pontius Pilate was dismissed in 36.

But his father-in-law Annas or Ananias was also called high priest. He held the post from 6 to 15 CE after the replacement of Herod's son Archelaus.. Although the Roman governor had replaced him with a member of his family, he still had been anointed as high priest so he certainly held a position of honour if not of formal authority.

In Acts 4.6 Luke lists the whole family: *'Annas the high priest, Caiaphas, John, and Alexander, and all who were of the high priestly family'.* All became high priests in turn apart from Alexander. John was high priest for 36-37 and again in 44.

3 How many trials?

Only John includes a late night investigation by Annas. He barely mentions a trial under Caiaphas, merely noting that Annas sent Jesus bound to Caiaphas, who sent him on to Pilate.

Mark tells of the major trial before the high priest, all the chief priests, the elders and scribes at night. The high priest is not named. Following a consultation at daybreak Jesus was sent over to Pilate.

Luke says that they led Jesus away to the high priest's house. Which one is not specified. At daybreak a trial was held before the assembly of the people, chief priests (plural) and scribes, and they sent Jesus to Pilate.

4 The timing

I take John's account to be as historical as the other gospels at this point. I assume that John was 'the other disciple who was known to the high priest'. He went straight into the courtyard and was able to bring Peter in as well. (John18.15). This would have been between 11.00 and midnight - when the first bugle sounded.

Then would have come the investigation in front of the former high priest. During this Peter would have been challenged by some of the high priest's servants. The second bugle call would have been heard at 3.00 a.m. This could have been the time that Jesus was taken to the house of Caiaphas, the official high priest.

There would then have been a gap of about three hours during which Caiaphas arranged a speedy trial to take place at daybreak, 6.00 a.m.

5 Recognition
It was hard to recognise people in the ancient world unless you knew them well. But there was no disguising Peter's northern accent. And the phrase, *"certainly you are one of them, for you are a Galilean",* betrays the unfriendly and dismissive attitude of ordinary people in Jerusalem to these troublesome pilgrims. *"Are you one of them?"* was not a friendly question.

REFLECTION

Simon Peter thought he was doing well when he refused to desert Jesus like the other ten disciples. Indeed he followed him right into the lion's den. John has the telling detail that the Jerusalem disciple (John?) knew the high priest's staff - and spoke with the right accent. He vouched for Peter to the gatekeeper, and then presumably went further inside, leaving Peter in the courtyard by the fire. I am not at all sure I would have had the courage to do what Peter did.

When challenged by the servant-girl about being one of Jesus' gang, which one of us would not respond as Peter did? Indeed, perhaps he did the right thing. In her book 'The Hiding Place' Corrie Ten Boom recounts how they hid Jews from the Nazis in the Second World War, and had no hesitation about lying when asked if they were hiding anyone. It happened again after Peter had left the warmth of the fire for the less conspicuous inner entrance. When it happened a third time, Peter's panic took over. *'He began to curse and to swear "I do not know the man.'* He had pushed himself too far and now could barely live with himself. *'He broke down and wept.'*

Peter is sometimes portrayed in sermons as weak, a bit of a coward. Not true. But none of us know where our breaking point might be. When we might say or do something which betrays our deepest values. In his 'Sermons in Solitary Confinement', (now republished as 'Alone with God') Richard Wurmbrand wrote movingly about his 14 years' experience in a Communist prison, including three years of solitary confinement thirty feet below ground. *"Be determined to cling to God, even if he slays you, even if he slays your faith. If you lose your faith, then remain faithlessly his."*

SUGGESTION

Read some account of Christians who suffer or have suffered persecution. There is no shortage of material.

Pray the Lord's Prayer, particularly *'Lead us not into temptation.'* This actually means 'Do not bring us to a time of trial'. And thank God that so far we have been spared the test.

MONDAY OF LENT 5 - ANNAS

Then the high priest questioned Jesus about his disciples and about his teaching. Jesus answered, 'I have spoken openly to the world; I have always taught in synagogues and in the temple, where all the Jews come together. I have said nothing in secret. Why do you ask me? Ask those who heard what I said to them; they know what I said.' When he had said this, one of the police standing nearby struck Jesus on the face, saying, 'Is that how you answer the high priest?' Jesus answered, 'If I have spoken wrongly, testify to the wrong. But if I have spoken rightly, why do you strike me?' Then Annas sent him bound to Caiaphas the high priest.

(John18.19-24)

THE SCENE

It was now the middle of the night, with the moon high overhead. The posse with their prisoner marched back up the hill, past the Pool of Bethesda, and up to the Antonia Fortress. Here the Roman officer and soldiers left them. The Temple guards took their prisoner through the gate leading to the grand Hasmonean palace. After a lengthy pause with men running into and out of the palace, Yeshua was taken into the main hall.

An imposing elderly white-bearded man was seated in the middle of various officials and servants. This was Anan whom the Romans had replaced as high priest over twenty years before, There was no sign of a secretary to take down evidence or of any of the members of the Great Council.

"So, Yeshua Ish-Natzaret, the preacher from Galil haGoyim, I am glad to see you, though obviously in unfortunate circumstances. You have made quite a name for yourself over this Pesach. Now, you are here on your own. Perhaps you can

208

tell us something about those who follow you. I believe that they are almost all from the Galil ha Goyim, is that true?"

Yeshua was silent.

"I can understand your wish not to incriminate any of your friends, but as the Great Council, we have a responsibility to safeguard the festival. It could lead to disaster if there was anything like a riot to happen. So please tell us, who are your close followers and where can we find them? It's important, even if only for their protection."

Again, no response.

"Well now, perhaps we can move to a different subject. Your teaching. I fear I have not had the opportunity to hear you in person, but as I understand it, you have made certain inflammatory statements which seem designed to turn people against us priests and leaders of the Temple. And yet the worship of the Temple is surely the heart of our nation, both here in Judaea and indeed all over the known world. Tell me, if you are a prophet, as some apparently claim, what is it you have said?"

At last Yeshua spoke.

"I have taught every day in the Temple throughout this week. Ask those who heard me."

A Temple guard on his left backhanded him hard on the right cheek, then gripped his jaw tightly in his hand.

"Is this how you answer back our high priest? Show some bloody respect!"

Yeshua shook his face free from the guard and said very deliberately,

"If I've spoken wrongly, make your statement as a witness. If not, why did you hit me?"

Anan intervened. *"Officer, I fully understand your frustration, but it won't help anyone if we allow this Galilean to rile us. As you know, my son-in-law Kayafa has been the official high priest for almost twenty years. He has enough experience to know how to deal with people who cause trouble. I only thought that we might be able to come to some more peaceable arrangement, unofficially."* He turned his attention to Yeshua. *"So, preacher, are you going to tell us what you have been speaking to the pilgrims here in Yerushalyim about?"*

Again, Yeshua was silent.

"Ah well, no one can say I didn't try. You'd better send him down to my son-in-law. He has a secure prison cell, small but certainly adequate for our preacher. Take him outside and look after him while I write a note to Yosef."

COMMENT

The trial, or rather investigation, in front of Annas, has a good claim to being the most factually reliable account of Jesus' last hours. This assumes that the writer of the gospel was the person who was known to the high priest and so was able to go inside the audience chamber without having questions asked. He records what he witnessed.

REFLECTION

Was Jesus tempted to describe his ministry and teaching to one of the most senior Jewish leaders? Annas was almost asking to be converted. For most of us it would be very hard to resist responding if only to correct someone's misperception. But of course it is a trap. Once you enter into any sort of dialogue, you implicitly recognise the possible validity of the other's point of view. Jesus was uncompromising in his teaching. That could only be defended by silence.

As the American writer Elbert Hubbard said, *"He who does not understand your silence will probably not understand your words."*

SUGGESTION

In his book on his experience of solitary confinement, Richard Wurmbrand writes to those *'who have the rare virtue of being silent and listening'.*

Take some minutes to sit in silence before God. Here are a few things I find helpful.

- Choose a period of time - 5, 10 or 20 minutes.

- Have a clock or watch in sight so when you start to panic you can check how long there is to go.

- Light a candle and use it as a visual focus point.

- Sit upright with both feet on the floor.

- Take three or four deep breaths, hold them for a count of four then gradually let it out for a count of five.

- Choose a single word that you can return to when your mind wanders, such as God - Love - Light - Jesus - Abba etc. Don't change the word during the silence.

- If some thoughts are very intrusive, like *"I must buy sausages",* write it down on a notepad and then let it go.

'Be still and know that I am God.' (Psalm 46.10)

TUESDAY OF LENT 5 - CAIAPHAS

The chief priests and the whole council were looking for testimony against Jesus to put him to death; but they found none. For many gave false testimony against him, and their testimony did not agree. Some stood up and gave false testimony against him, saying, 'We heard him say, "I will destroy this temple that is made with hands, and in three days I will build another, not made with hands." ' But even on this point their testimony did not agree. Then the high priest stood up before them and asked Jesus, 'Have you no answer? What is it that they testify against you?' But he was silent and did not answer.

(Mark 14.55-61)

THE SCENE

Kayafa's palace was alive with activity. Flaming torches at the main entrance lit up the street, with more of them as well as charcoal braziers in the courtyard. It was crowded with uniformed troops and household servants, hurrying on various errands. The guards from Anan's palace handed Yeshua over to Kayafas' captain of security, who pushed him down a couple steps into a small windowless dungeon. Yeshua was left in pitch darkness in a bare stone cell.

A couple of hours later, the door opened and he was taken up to the inner courtyard. Night was beginning to lighten; you could see the black of buildings against the slightly lighter blue-black of the night sky. Two guards stood next to Yeshua and watched the comings and goings of the palace servants, priests in white tunics and Torah-teachers in black cloaks. The bugle call from the Antonia for the early morning watch could just be heard as a servant came out and told the captain to

213

bring the prisoner to the small hall at the back of the palace complex.

Two guards stood on either side of Yeshua with the captain alongside. The hall they were in was not large enough to hold the whole of the Great Council. The Hall of Polished Stone in the Temple was their official location. But there was plenty of room for the two dozen Temple aristocrats and leading priests to sit on stools in a shallow semi-circle along the long wall of the room with the High Priest in the centre. The captain smiled grimly to himself. He recognised that most of them were members of just six priestly families. *"The man's not got a chance,"* he thought to himself.

Kayafa, an imposing man in his mid-fifties, tall and with a full black beard, stood up and addressed Yeshua.

"Prisoner, you have been arrested on a number of charges. Witnesses will be brought in for us to consider the evidence. But first, your name?"

Yeshua was silent.

"Ach, is this your stupid game? Can anyone here witness to the name of the prisoner?"

"I met him in the Temple, when he ridiculed us priests and Torah-teachers. His name is Yeshua Bar-Yosef."

"I believe he is normally called Yeshua Ish-Natzarit, because that is his home village."

"He also goes by the name of Yeshua Bar-Miryam, for reasons we can only guess at."

A ripple of laughter ran round the hall. Kayafa
spoke again.

*"Well, Yeshua, we can only speculate why you need so many
names. It doesn't seem to me a very honest procedure. But I
suppose it is not illegal, so let us quickly pass on. Bring in the
first witness."*

Kayafa sat down. A man wearing an embroidered cloak
and with an avaricious expression on his face entered.

"Your name?"

"El'ichud Bar-Z'khariyah, your Grace."

"Welcome. What charges do you bring against the prisoner?"

*"For over twenty years I have been faithfully changing defiled
money into sacred coinage so that worshippers can properly
buy their sacrifices. No one in authority has ever complained
about my business. But four days ago, this Galilean stormed
into the sacred Temple, threw over my table and the tables of
my colleagues and ordered us to leave. I only did so because
of the scores of his supporters who were frankly threatening,
and I did not want our holy house to be desecrated by
violence. I lost a great deal of honestly acquired money
through this mountebank!"*

*"So - your charges are incitement to violence, destruction of
property and desecration of the Temple?"*

*"Yes, your Grace. And I have several friends outside wishing
to make the same charges."*

"Yeshua, how do you plead to these charges?"

Silence.

"Thank you El'ichud. Please withdraw, while we discuss your evidence."

When the merchant had left, Kayafa addressed the Council.

"What the merchant said is undoubtedly true, but it will hardly serve our purpose. The most we could sentence this pretended prophet to is a flogging and time in prison. With thousands of his fellow-Galileans here in the city we have to act decisively, and fast. They will be beginning to gather in the Temple in a couple of hours. Do you agree?"

All murmured their assent.

"Very well. Call the next witness."

COMMENT

1 Bedroom talk

In 'Jesus the Troublemaker' I imagined a conversation between Caiaphas and his wife at the end of the evening. Here is an an extract:

"I had only a few hours to get everything fixed. I got your father to use delaying tactics, which he did with his usual consummate skill."

"He's great, my Dad"

"Indeed he is. But he didn't get very far with this Yeshua, so he sent him off down to us before anything was ready. Fortunately, we had an empty dungeon to store our Galilean prophet in. I had determined that the trial would be here and not in the Temple

- far too many people around, and my hall is big enough for a small Council meeting. By first light I'd been able to summon a sufficient number of reliable council members for the trial and had got the guards here to round up some promising witnesses."

"So after all your preparations, did it go smoothly?"

"Not exactly. The witnesses were uniformly hopeless, and I was in danger of losing the support of some of the council members. But looking carefully at this Yeshua, I thought that there might still be a way. He seemed just the type to hang himself out of sheer pride. So I asked him, 'Are you Ha Mashiach?'"

2 The Dungeon

Archaeologists have discovered a dungeon in Caiaphas' palace, so I imagined that is where they kept Jesus until the trial started. I remember visiting an ancient dungeon on the Via Dolorosa (though not the one which housed Jesus). I went inside and the door swung shut. The sudden blackness was very alarming! I can easily envisage Jesus being left in darkness for two or three hours while Caiaphas did his best to fix the trial and waited for first light.

3 Morning

Sunrise was about 6.30 at the beginning of April, with first light half an hour before. According to early Jewish tradition it was illegal to hold a trial at night, so, following Luke's gospel, I believe the trial under Caiaphas would have started at first light at 6.00. The priests and council members were used to getting up early, because priests in the Temple cast lots at first light to determine who would carry out which of the tasks of the day.

4 The Witnesses

We are told many stood up and gave false testimony. In my book I imagined what these might have been. It would not have been difficult to drum up some prosecution witnesses from the traders in the Temple. I also included a scribe who tried to twist Jesus' words into incitement to rebellion. My favourite is 'Tol' who firmly believed that Jesus was a magician who had learned his dark arts in Egypt. This is a slander that was written in the Talmud, c.300 CE. Finally two good witnesses who unfortunately disagreed between themselves. Had Caiaphas had even one day longer to arrange things, the testimony of witnesses would have been much more convincing..

REFLECTION

It is heartening when a self-serving administration fails to run smoothly or is called to account. It is a miraculous moment when a totalitarian regime collapses.

Leipzig in Germany is a great city to visit. Not only is it the home of J S Bach. It also lit the spark in 1989 which brought down the Communist government.

For several years the pastor of the St Nicolas church (Nikolaikirche) had led 'peace prayers' in the church on Mondays. Early in 1989 the numbers in church grew to several hundred, until in September they spilled out on to the square outside, still holding lighted candles. The Communist government had violently put down demonstrations a month earlier. Now they decided to put down the demonstration outside the Nikolaikirche once and for all. They drafted in 7,000 extra soldiers and police. But that evening 70,000 turned up. The crowd walked entirely peacefully, chanting "We are the people" and the soldiers and police just stood aside. A month later the government and Politburo resigned and the Berlin Wall came down. A member of the Politburo said later, *"We had prepared for all eventualities. The only factors we had not taken into account were prayers and candles."*

SUGGESTION

Can you think of an occasion when a politician or government has been less than honest? (Do not write on both sides of the paper at once).

A Chinese proverb says, *"It is better to light a candle than to curse the darkness."*

At night put a lighted candle in the window and look at it while praying for the government and nation.

WEDNESDAY OF LENT 5 – "I AM"

Again the high priest asked him, 'Are you the Messiah, the Son of the Blessed One?' Jesus said, 'I am; and you will see the Son of Man seated at the right hand of the Power, and coming with the clouds of heaven.'

Then the high priest tore his clothes and said, 'Why do we still need witnesses? You have heard his blasphemy! What is your decision?' All of them condemned him as deserving death.

Some began to spit on him, to blindfold him, and to strike him, saying to him, 'Prophesy!' The guards also took him over and beat him.

(Mark 14.61-65)

THE SCENE

Kayafa looked straight at the calm figure of Yeshua in front of him, noting his erect stature, his fearless gaze, as if he, Yeshua, was the one in authority here in the hall, here in Yerushalayim, here in Yisrael.

"Maybe this will work," Kayafa said to himself. With great dignity, he stood up. You could have heard a pin drop. Kayafa and Yeshua looked straight into each other's eyes. Kayafa said quietly, almost conversationally,

"Yeshua Ish-Natzaret, are you Ha Mashiach - the Anointed - the Son of the Blessed One?"

There was a pause and everyone held their breath.

Yeshua said, equally quietly in Aramaic, *"'Ena ena - I am."*

The council chamber erupted into shocked cries from the whole assembly. Yeshua's voice rose above them all. *"AND YOU WILL SEE THE SON OF MAN SEATED AT THE RIGHT HAND OF THE MOST HIGH AND COMING ON THE CLOUDS OF HEAVEN!"*

Kayafa gestured for the noise to abate and then theatrically tore the top half of his blue silk tunic in two.

"You have heard the blasphemy? That such things should be uttered in Israel! What is your verdict?"

"ISH MAVEH!" *"DEATH,"* was the almost unanimous shout.

"My lord", whispered the secretary, *"Is this strictly legal? Blasphemy means stoning. That might be difficult in a city full of pilgrims."*

"I know. Don't fear, he said he was Ha-Mashiach - God's anointed. That's a political claim. We'll take him over to the Romans. I had a word with Pilatus last night. Sometimes even the Romans have their uses."

COMMENT

1 What did Jesus say?
What did Jesus actually say that got him condemned?

- Mark has the high priest's question as being: *"Are you the Messiah, the son of the Blessed One?"* to which Jesus replies, *"I am"*
- Matthew gives Jesus' answer as, *"You have said so."*
- Luke has a different question, *"Are you, then, the Son of God?"*, to which Jesus replies, *"You say that I am."*

I think that Mark's account is the most likely one to be original. I can understand why the early Jewish Christians could feel uncomfortable in saying the most sacred words in the Torah, and changed them into a politer way if saying 'yes'. And Luke does the same. Luke's question has also been changed to one that makes sense to a Gentile audience rather than a Jewish one.

2 What were his actual words?

- 'I am' is English.
- 'Ego eimi' is Greek, the language the New Testament was written in.
- 'Ehyeh' is Hebrew, part of the phrase 'Ehyeh asher ehyeh' - 'I am who I am', which God declared to Moses at the burning bush (Exodus 3.14). It is not the same as 'Yahweh' or 'Jehovah' which is used in the following verse and means something related to 'he is'.
- 'Ena ena' (or 'ena hu') is 'I am' in Aramaic, Jesus' native language. This is the phrase used in the ancient Syriac version of Mark's gospel.

So: did Jesus continue to use the language which the trial had been conducted in? Was the claim then seen as effectively blasphemous?

Or did Jesus slip into the sacred language of Hebrew, so claiming some sort of equality with God?

When I wrote the scene, I decided after much hesitation to use the Aramaic phrase.

3 Flinging down the gauntlet

Jesus immediately announces the imminent arrival of the heavenly Messiah. He uses the phrase 'the Son of Man' which among other uses also meant 'I'. We have met this prophecy before , in Jesus' teaching to his disciples on the Mount of

Olives. It was a claim that was impossible for the Sanhedrin to ignore. I then used the phrase 'Ish Maveh', literally 'man of death', the Talmud's formula for the death penalty.

4 Beaten up

There is a hidden brutality at the heart of humanity. When we think of those who have suffered, whether victims of war or torture or domestic abuse, there are also those who are killers, torturers, abusers. People's moral barriers against hateful actions can broken down by permission from those in authority, or by the 'canteen culture' of group think, or by unprocessed rage. As soon as Jesus was condemned, these behaviours burst out. Here is my suggestion in 'Jesus the Troublemaker' of how the soldiers at Annas' palace behaved:

> Four guards walked Yeshua out of the hall and tripped him up, so he fell flat on the marble pavement. They all laughed.
>
> *"Hey, guys, we can have a bit of fun with our prophet. Someone put a blindfold on him."*
>
> They hauled him to his feet, wrapped a cloth over his eyes and pushed his back against a wall. One punched him hard in the stomach.
>
> *"Come on, prophet, tell me what my name is. Don't know? Maybe this will help."*
>
> Another punch.
>
> *"He's a bit sleepy, ain't he? Maybe a slap will wake him up."* Two slaps, left and right, followed. *"Come on, prophet, tell us the winner in the chariot race tomorrow, I could do with some winnings."* Silence. *"Ah, you spoilsport. Take that!"*

A fist struck his chin." *Hey, go easy Matt, don't knock him out! We don't want to have to carry him through the city."*

How could I write that? Because at some level I could do it.

REFLECTION

1 When Jesus replied to the question 'Are you the Messiah the Son of the Blessed One', he replied 'I am'. The response was immediate rejection.

How do we respond to his claim? If we don't find it shocking, it's because we have sanitised it with two millennia of church, art and music. It means taking with the utmost seriousness the things he said and did during the three years before this event. *Before the cross and resurrection!* Particularly in the gospels of Mark and Luke. It means taking a radically different approach to money, to society, to prayer. St Paul got it:

Whatever gains I had, these I have come to regard as dung because of the surpassing value of knowing Christ Jesus my Lord...".
        (Philippians 3.7 - the twelfth word correctly translated!)

2 The other side of this story is to recognise what evil we could be capable of. And to admit it.

SUGGESTION

Find a good picture of Jesus, perhaps an early icon like the one in St Catherine's monastery in Sinai, Egypt. There are plenty of images on the world wide web. Spend some minutes being present in front of it, saying quietly to yourself, 'Jesus, Lord.'

End with the Lord's Prayer.

THURSDAY OF LENT 5 - PILATE

*A*s soon as it was morning, the chief priests held a consultation with the elders and scribes and the whole council. They bound Jesus, led him away, and handed him over to Pilate. Pilate asked him, 'Are you the King of the Jews?' He answered him, 'You say so.' Then the chief priests accused him of many things. Pilate asked him again, 'Have you no answer? See how many charges they bring against you.' But Jesus made no further reply, so that Pilate was amazed.

(Mark 15.1-5)

THE SCENE

Kayafa had changed into a white silk tunic and a royal blue cloak, impressively ornamented with gold, jewels and pearls. He walked at the head of a group of six priests and Temple aristocrats in their best white linen, followed by the guards marching ahead of and behind Yeshua. They walked along Market Street, with the people gawping at the unusual procession taking place on the First day of Unleavened Bread. Directly opposite the Market Square was the heavily fortified entrance to the two palaces. The guard on duty saluted Kayafa respectfully and sent a messenger to the procurator's HQ. The group turned right into the central space between the two palaces, half a mile long, and walked to the Praetorium at the end. They halted in front of the 25-foot-wide porch leading to the Governor's residence, with the enormous Hippichus tower looming overhead. A slave came out, bowed respectfully and said that the governor would be out in a minute. A couple of slaves brought out a gilded wooden chair with sloping arms and carved insignia of Rome, and a bronze table with three legs, and placed them in the middle of the porch. Another slave brought in a silver goblet and a small jug of wine. A secretary brought in papyrus, reed pen and ink, a clay shorthand tablet and a wooden writing mat.

Pontius Pilatus, every inch a military man, strode out of the Praetorium's gateway, wearing a short white toga over a white tunic with two narrow vertical purple-red stripes. He walked over to Kayafa and shook his hand.

"Xairé,* your Grace."

"Xairé, Excellency."

Pilatus sat down and looked enquiringly at the high priest.

"Well, High Priest, I assume this is the person we have spoken about. Perhaps you can enlighten me about the exact charges against him."

"Excellency, I assure you we would not have bothered you at this early hour had it not been a matter of some gravity. I have just come from a meeting of the Great Council - small, but quorate - and it was our almost unanimous decision that this man needs to suffer the supreme penalty of being a threat to the Empire. To deal with the prisoner is in our view essential to keeping good order in the land."

"High Priest, I don't need you to tell me how to maintain order. What I do need is for you to tell me why he is such a threat."

"Of course, Excellency. Brother Sila, please be so kind as to summarise the findings of the Council."

"Absolutely, your Grace. Excellency. This man has been a disturber of the peace for many months. He even *sacrilegiously brought violence into the Temple itself only four days ago."*

"I am aware of that. I do get daily reports from my officer in the Antonia. He reports that the Temple since that incident has been unusually peaceful."

"Yes, Excellency, but he does make inflammatory statements. For example, only two days ago he made a coded comment inviting people to stop paying their imperial taxes."

"Coded? In what way coded?"

The priest Sila blushed with embarrassment and could not think of a reply.

"Prisoner, perhaps you can enlighten me. What were these coded comments about not paying the imperial taxes?"

Yeshua looked straight at Pilatus but said nothing. Kayafa interjected,

"Excellency, we found this self-same stubbornness when we in the Great Council were interrogating him. Carry on, brother Sila."

"Excellency, he has created upset all over the province. He does not keep the Shabbat but insists on carrying on his alleged healing campaigns which simply sow division and create unrealistic expectations..."

"Priest, I am deeply uninterested in your religious disputes. I shall therefore..."

"Excellency, I apologise for interrupting you, but the most serious charge has only just now come to light. In the meeting

227

of the Great Council he claimed to be - er – 'Ha Mashiach…"

Kayafa broke in smoothly.

"Xristos, Excellency, the Anointed. It is a special royal title for us. Judas the Galilean who raised a revolt in the year of the census under the noble legate Quirinius, made a similar claim. His insurrection had to be put down by force with considerable loss of life."

"So, High Priest, tell me in plain words what 'Xristos' means to you and your people."

"The best I can say is, 'Basileus Iudaeōn' - the King of the Jews.

"Really? The King of the Jews? All of them? Here? Alexandria? Rome? All right, I now have something to ask him. Ieesoo - are you the King of the Jews?"

Yeshua calmly replied in Greek, *"It is as you say."*

* Xairé, meaning 'Rejoice', was the standard Greek greeting.

COMMENT

1 The Gospel Accounts
The gospels have slightly different detail about the trial before Pilate. But all four agree that the prime charge made against Jesus in front of Pilate was that he claimed to be the King of the Jews. And that Jesus accepted the charge! My reconstruction above relies on the gospels of John 18.28-33 and Luke 23.22.

2 The Character of Pilate
The character of Pontius Pilate in the gospels seems be one of a fair-minded even liberal magistrate. This is at odds

from what we know of him from other historical sources. There we find him to be, in the words of Philo, the Jewish philosopher of Alexandria, *"naturally inflexible and stubborn"* (Leg. ad Gaium 301f). When confronted with a difficult situation he was only too ready to use force to solve it. When a crowd of Jews protested against his using money from the Temple treasury to build an aqueduct for Jerusalem, he sent soldiers into the crowd dressed as civilians but with clubs under their cloaks. At his signal they proceeded to beat the people causing mass panic and many deaths, in the tradition of riot police everywhere. He used similar tactics to crush an armed protest in Samaria in 36, an action which prompted his recall to Rome in disgrace. Jesus spoke of *'the Galileans whose blood Pilate had mingled with their sacrifices'* (Luke 13.1). Pilate was governor of Judaea and Samaria with the rank of Prefect from 26 to 36 CE. He may eventually have retired to his home province of Umbria in central Italy.

Reflecting on the evidence, I concluded that the person most like him was Brigadier-General Dyer. He orchestrated the Amritsar massacre in India in 1919, when he had his troops open fire on an unarmed crowd in an enclosed public square because they were violating his order of no public assemblies. Between 380 and 1,000 men, women and children were killed. It would have been worse if the armoured cars with their machine guns had been able to get through the narrow gateways. To the end of his life, Dyer maintained that he had done the right thing, stating that his act *"was not to disperse the meeting but to punish the Indians for disobedience."*

Pilate came from a wealthy family and was almost certainly a military man, perhaps with special skill with the javelin or 'pilus'. He had the senator Sejanus as a patron, who fell into disfavour around the time of the trial of Jesus, so he had lost his protector with the emperor. In 36 he probably retired to his home province in central Italy. I aimed to sum up his character in the remark he makes to Caiaphas, *"High priest, I don't need you to tell me how to maintain order."*

3 The King of the Jews
When Jesus essentially replied 'Yes' to the question, "Are you the King of the Jews?" why did not Pilate immediately order his execution?

Pilate was not completely unaware of Jesus. He certainly knew of Jesus' takeover of the Outer Court of the Temple four days previously. He also knew that the Sanhedrin had not asked for Roman intervention. As far as he knew there was no hint of armed insurrection or of any illegal activity by Jesus or his followers. It would seem that the mere claim of being 'the king of the Jews' was not enough to condemn someone. It could be another of these intra-Jewish squabbles. For example, the 'teacher of righteousness', the head of the Essene sect, would have nothing to do with the person they called 'the wicked priest' in Jerusalem, in other words Annas and his family.

There may be a parallel with an incident that happened thirty years later in 62. Josephus in his 'The Jewish War' tells of a certain Jesus son of Ananias who 'kept speaking against Jerusalem and the sanctuary'. The Jewish authorities were desperate to get rid of him and, when other sanctions failed, they had to refer him to the Roman governor Albinus. Albinus had Jesus bar-Ananias flayed to the bone with scourges, then released him as a madman. Was that what Pilate intended to do with Jesus?

4 Jerusalem syndrome
In 2000 an article was published by the British Journal of Psychiatry:

'Since 1980, Jerusalem's psychiatrists have encountered an ever-increasing number of tourists who, upon arriving in Jerusalem, suffer psychotic decompensation. In view of the consistently high incidence of this phenomenon, it was decided to channel all such cases to one central facility - the Kfar Shaul Mental Health Centre - for psychological counselling, psychiatric intervention and, if deemed necessary, admission to hospital. Over the course of 13 years (1980-1993), 1200 tourists with severe, Jerusalem-generated mental problems have been referred to this facility. Of these, 470 were admitted to hospital. On average, 100 such tourists are seen annually, 40 of them requiring admission to hospital.'

Similar incidents were recorded back in the 15th century. Perhaps there were similar incidents during the great Jewish feasts at the Temple at the time of Jesus. The case of the man scourged by Albinus indicates the possibility. Might this explain Pilate's unwillingness to take the accusations of the high priest at face value? The problem for Pilate was that Jesus appeared peaceable but also completely sane.

REFLECTION

The liberties and limits of power

We have the general idea that the government can do anything it likes. In western democracies there are constitutional constraints, and the need to be aware of the next general election. In totalitarian states public opinion is carefully monitored. For instance, in Nazi Germany the SS carefully monitored public opinion and were concerned when in 1943 Hitler was starting to become unpopular with the rank and file.

Of course government do have real ability to do things and shape events, but there are innumerable occasions when it is very hard to make decisions. In 2010 during the Conservative/Lib Dem coalition government, Nick Clegg was asked what it was like being Deputy Prime Minister. He replied, *"It is like being slowly lobotomised."*

Could we sometimes look behind the news to the people - good, bad and indifferent - who make up the news?

SUGGESTION

Take a couple of politicians about whom we have strong negative feelings, and find out a bit about their backgrounds. Not to agree with them, but to get a bit more understanding that could help us pray for them. And don't forget your local M.P.

FRIDAY OF LENT 5 - HEROD

*T*he chief priests were insistent and said, 'He stirs up the people by teaching throughout all Judea, from Galilee where he began even to this place.'

When Pilate heard this, he asked whether the man was a Galilean. And when he learned that he was under Herod's jurisdiction, he sent him off to Herod, who was himself in Jerusalem at that time. When Herod saw Jesus, he was very glad, for he had been wanting to see him for a long time, because he had heard about him and was hoping to see him perform some sign. He questioned him at some length, but Jesus gave him no answer. The chief priests and the scribes stood by, vehemently accusing him. Even Herod with his soldiers treated him with contempt and mocked him; then he put an elegant robe on him, and sent him back to Pilate. That same day Herod and Pilate became friends with each other; before this they had been enemies.

(Luke 23.5-12)

THE SCENE

A letter from Pilate to Herod

'Pontius Pilatus, procurator of Judaea and Samaria, to the honourable Herod Antipas, Tetrarch of Galilee and Peraea.

Xairé. I wish you health and good fortune.

I have just finished questioning a prisoner brought to me by the high priest Caiaphas. His name is Iēsous and he has been accused of disturbing the peace in various ways, or rather of disturbing our good friends of the Sanhedrin. Apparently, he has claimed publicly to be the Xristos - the Anointed - about which I know little. However, in my questioning I have discovered that he is in fact a citizen of Galilee and therefore

233

comes under your jurisdiction. I am sending him over to you for your decision on his future. Please give my regards to your lady wife Herodias.

The eighteenth year of Tiberius Caesar, the seventh day of Aprilios.'

A letter from Herod to Pilate

"Herod Antipas, Tetrarch of Galilee and Peraea to his Excellency Pontius Pilatus, Procurator of Judaea and Samaria.

Greeting. I thank the God of our fathers daily for your firm governance of the Province. And I specially thank you for sending me the interesting prisoner Iēsoun,   and your courtesy in acknowledging my interest in those who live in the territory appointed for me.

I was interested to meet him, but sadly he's like one of the mute swans on my ornamental lakes - all feathers and no voice. However, on learning of his claim to be the Xristos, I believe that he now comes under your jurisdiction. Part of the claim traditionally includes provenance from the town of Bethlehem, the city of David in the territory of Judah. I therefore return him to you with my compliments.

I would also like to invite you, my dear Pilatus, for dinner in my palace here at the end of the present feast. We shall then be able to enjoy decent bread. We have for too long allowed a few local misunderstandings to cloud what should, I believe, be a harmonious working relationship. I wish you the best of health, and as much serenity as this city allows.

The eighteenth year of Tiberius Caesar, the seventh day of Aprilios in the morning.

COMMENT

1 Location, location, location

Only Luke mentions the interrogation of Jesus by Herod
Antipas, in between Pilate's two attempts to resolve matters.
I used to think that this was unrealistic. I could not see how
a half hour's walk in both directions could fit the overall
timetables for Jesus' trials and crucifixion. I then realised,
in John Robinson's words in 'The Priority of John' p. 267
*"that it is overwhelmingly probable that the Praetorium (military
headquarters) was in Herod's palace and not in the Antonia".*

Herod's palace was effectively an enormous castle stretching
a mile along the Western wall of Jerusalem with its own
protective wall facing the city. It was built by Herod I who
died in 4 BCE. It enclosed not one but two palaces, one at
either end. On Herod I's death, his son Archelaus inherited
the whole complex. When in 6 CE Archelaus was deposed
by Rome for his bad government, Herod Antipas, ruler
of Galilee, was given the southern one. The northern one
became the Roman army barracks, and the seat of the
governor whenever he stayed in Jerusalem.

Between the two palaces was an enormous piazza, half
a mile long, raised fifteen feet above street level (hence
'Gabbatha') and paved with a mosaic pavement (hence
'lithōstratos' (John 19.13). So for Pilate to send Jesus to Herod
only involved a ten minute walk.

2 Herod Antipas

Herod Antipas was a much more interesting figure than
the Bible suggests. He was the youngest son of Herod I, on
whose death he was made the ruler of Galilee and part of
Transjordan. He held the title of tetrarch, which means ruler
of a quarter of Herod's lands. He ruled his territory for over
forty years until he was obliged to retire in disgrace in 39 CE.

He was quite a good ruler. He kept the peace, in particular by not offending Jewish sensibilities by having no images on his coins. He encouraged the economic development of Galilee by building both Sepphoris and Tiberias. He was religious and superstitious but not devout:.

'Now Herod the ruler heard about all that had taken place, and he was perplexed, because it was said by some that John had been raised from the dead, by some that Elijah had appeared, and by others that one of the ancient prophets had arisen. Herod said, 'John I beheaded; but who is this about whom I hear such things?' And he tried to see him. (Luke 9.7-9)

Herod himself had sent men who arrested John, bound him, and put him in prison on account of Herodias. For John had been telling Herod, 'It is not lawful for you to have your brother's wife.' Herod feared John, knowing that he was a righteous and holy man, and he protected him. When he heard him, he was greatly perplexed; and yet he liked to listen to him. (Mark 17, 20)

Some Pharisees came and said to Jesus, 'Get away from here, for Herod wants to kill you.' He said to them, 'Go and tell that fox for me, "Listen, I am casting out demons and performing cures today and tomorrow, and on the third day I finish my work. (Luke 13.31-32)

What did Pilate expect when he sent Jesus over to Herod? My guess is that he thought Herod would treat him the same as John the Baptist - march him out of Jerusalem and imprison him, like John the Baptist, in one of his castles by the Dead Sea. Problem solved.

3 Herod's questions

Luke tells us that Herod questioned Jesus 'at some length'. What about? I guess five possibilities:

a) The remarkable healing of the son of one of his officials in Capernaum (John 4.46-54);

b) The Orthodox disapproval of the building of Tiberias over a disused Jewish cemetery;

c) the execution of John the Baptist;

d) Jesus' opinion of him as 'a fox'.

e) General questions about his teaching and his disciples.

Jesus answer to all Herod's questions and self-justification was the same - silence.

REFLECTION

On one of my trips to Israel I visited the Lake of Galilee on my own. I climbed up to the top of the hill to the Church of the Beatitudes. It was a beautiful sunny day, and I sat in the open colonnade overlooking the inland sea. While there I read through the first nine chapters of the Gospel of Mark. From this vantage point you could trace virtually all of Jesus' movements: down from Nazareth, through the lakeside towns ,across the lake and back, and up towards the north and back. What was striking was also where Jesus did not go. Only six miles away was the important town of Tiberias. As far as we know, Jesus never set foot there.

Why? Perhaps because Jesus saw very little difference between Herod's token Judaism allied with a major dose of Greek culture and being an out-and-out Gentile. Worse in some ways, because Jesus did go to the Gentiles' coastal city of Tyre when he wanted a break. (Mark 7.24). He specifically warned his disciples against *"the yeast of the Pharisees and the yeast of Herod."* (Mark 8.15)

Was Jesus' silence before Herod a way of saying, as in Revelation 3.15-16, *"because you are lukewarm, and neither cold nor hot, I am about to spit you out of my mouth."*

SUGGESTION

Pray for those in positions of authority, that they may respect human dignity and seek the common good. Pray particularly for the government, the opposition, your own MP, and your local council.

SATURDAY OF LENT 5 – PILATE AND THE CROWD

Pilate then called together the chief priests, the leaders, and the people, and said to them, 'You brought me this man as one who was perverting the people; and here I have examined him in your presence and have not found this man guilty of any of your charges against him. Neither has Herod, for he sent him back to us. Indeed, he has done nothing to deserve death. I will therefore have him flogged and release him.' Then they all shouted out together, 'Away with this fellow! Release Barabbas for us!' (This was a man who had been put in prison for an insurrection that had taken place in the city, and for murder.) Pilate, wanting to release Jesus, addressed them again; but they kept shouting, 'Crucify, crucify him!' A third time he said to them, 'Why, what evil has he done? I have found in him no ground for the sentence of death; I will therefore have him flogged and then release him.' But they kept urgently demanding with loud shouts that he should be crucified; and their voices prevailed. So Pilate gave his verdict that their demand should be granted. He released the man they asked for, the one who had been put in prison for insurrection and murder, and he handed Jesus over as they wished.

(Luke 23.13-25)

THE SCENE

The group arrived at the Praetorium entrance. One of the high priest's guards handed Herod's letter to one of the soldiers on duty who took it inside to the governor. After a few minutes, a soldier came out to the group and said that the prefect wanted to interrogate the prisoner privately. As he escorted Yeshua inside, Kayafa gritted his teeth in annoyance and frustration. He ordered one of the guards,

"Go and find the captain and get whoever is in the Market Square inside on the Palace Pavement as soon as possible.

239

> *And remind him that one prisoner due for execution today is the Zealot Barabbas. He's popular. Tell the crowd to shout for him. After fifteen years, I think I know how our esteemed governor's mind works. We've got to get this thing done."*

COMMENTS

The Gospel Accounts

The order of events according to Mark (15.3-15):
1. Jesus makes no answer to any of the accusations against him
2. The crowd ask for the release of Barabbas.
3. Pilate suggests he release Jesus of Nazareth instead.
4. The crowd ask for Barabbas
5. They demand that Jesus be crucified.
6. Jesus is flogged
7. Jesus is led out to execution.

The order of events according to Luke (23.13-25):
1. Pilate calls together the chief priests, leaders and the people.
2. Pilate proposes to flog Jesus and release him.
3. The crowd ask for the release of Barabbas.
4. The crowd demand Jesus be crucified.
5. Pilate agrees to do what the crowd want.

The order of events according to John (18.33 - 19.16):
1. Pilate questions Jesus inside the Praetorium/military headquarters.
2. Pilate offers the crowd the choice between releasing Barabbas or Jesus.
3. Jesus is flogged, then comes out with a crown of thorns and a royal cloak.
4. Pilate tries to release Jesus
5. The chief priests tell Pilate that Jesus called himself

Son of God, and that if he lets Jesus go, they can report him to the emperor.

6   Pilate makes a final appeal, then orders Jesus to be crucified.

The order of events according to Matthew:
These are the same as in Mark, with the extra detail of the dream of Pilate's wife, *"Have nothing to do with that innocent man."* (Matthew 27.19). Without any additional support, I regard this story as a product of Christian imagination, not of actual events.

All the gospels tell the same story with two main differences.

The Flogging
Mark says that Jesus was flogged as part of his sentence of crucifixion. John puts it in front of Pilate's second appeal to the crowd, and Luke implies that it happened there as the formal punishment: *"I will have him flogged and release him."* (Luke 23.16). In view of how the Procurator Albinus treated Jesus, son of Ananias, in 62 CE, this is a likely scenario.

The Blackmail
Only John implies that what finally changed Pilate's mind was the threat to report him to Tiberius Caesar: *'If you release this man, you are no friend of the emperor. Everyone who claims to be a king sets himself against the emperor.'* (John 19.12). This makes sense if Pilate's intention was to follow normal procedure and have Jesus flogged and released. (The flogging was no joke. Some men died under that punishment). The chief priests were set on achieving a permanent solution.

The Crowd

Innumerable sermons have spoken of the fickleness of the crowd that shouted "Hosanna to the Son of David!" on Sunday and five days later were shouting "Crucify him!" With the accompanying question: "Have you ever been fickle?" It is a natural temptation to the preacher to want to make his congregation feel guilt. We all like to make some impact when we speak to others, and inducing feelings of guilt is the easiest way to do that. But it really is unnecessary.

What seems to me obvious is that we are talking about two different crowds. The one on Palm Sunday, made up of pilgrims from the Galil; and the Jerusalem crowd, made up of angry traders, plus families, clients and employees of the great priestly families, and all who resented the traffic jams caused by Jesus when he took over the Outer Court of the Temple - *their* Temple. They just wanted the Galilean preacher out of the way - permanently.

REFLECTION

In 'Brave New World Revisited' Aldous Huxley wrote, *'A crowd is chaotic, has no purpose of its own and is capable of anything except intelligent action and realistic thinking. Assembled in a crowd, people lose their powers of reasoning and their capacity for moral choice. Their suggestibility is increased to the point where they cease to have any judgment or will of their own. They become very excitable, they lose all sense of individual or collective responsibility, they are subject to sudden accesses of rage, enthusiasm and panic.'* This is a good description of the crowd that shouted "Crucify!"

Fundamental to the psychology of a crowd is the conviction, conscious or subconscious, of belonging to a tribe. When we feel our tribe is under threat, we easily act irrationally with the aim of defending our tribe against the outsider. Classic examples have been the Falklands War against Argentina, when there were loud calls to boycott Argentinian corned beef; or the American response to France's refusal to join in the Second Gulf War by renaming 'French Fries' as 'Freedom Fries'; or anything associated with Brexit, for or against.

It is easy for us to be sucked into irrational attitudes and actions unless we are clear about where they come from. That needs self-awareness of the tribes we consciously or unconsciously belong to, national, political, religious or other.

SUGGESTION

Take a few moments to stop and reflect on what kinds of groups we naturally feel linked with, and what kinds of groups we feel separate from. Pray that God may give us insight into those we don't naturally relate to. Try to learn something new from them.

HOLY WEEK

CRUCIFIXION

Golgotha/Skull Hill

PALM SUNDAY - SCOURGING

So Pilate, wishing to satisfy the crowd, released Barabbas for them; and after flogging Jesus, he handed him over to be crucified. Then the soldiers led him into the courtyard of the palace (that is, the governor's headquarters); and they called together the whole cohort. And they clothed him in a purple cloak; and after twisting some thorns into a crown, they put it on him. And they began saluting him, 'Hail, King of the Jews!' They struck his head with a reed, spat upon him, and knelt down in homage to him. After mocking him, they stripped him of the purple cloak and put his own clothes on him. Then they led him out to crucify him.

(Mark 15.15-20)

THE SCENE

Yeshua was led by two soldiers down the stairs to the paved central courtyard. It was almost always in shade because the two-storey building on all four sides. At one side stood a free-standing pillar with iron manacles fixed to the stone, eight feet above the ground. Yeshua stood silent as they stripped him of the purple cloak, his own woollen cloak, his long-sleeved tunic and even his loin cloth. He allowed his hands to be locked in the manacles without a curse or a complaint. Then nothing, until the tramp of a hundred pairs of heavy-soled sandals echoed round the courtyard. Orders were shouted by the centurion and a hundred soldiers stood in ranks along one wall.

The senior centurion barked *"Men, you've been called here to witness a historic achievement. The prisoner, who claims to be the Xristos, or the king of this god-forsaken province, has been captured without a drop of blood being spilt. The procurator has sentenced him to crucifixion, so now comes the first part of his penalty, forty lashes. Who's going to*

247

volunteer for the first eight?" Hands shot up, but discipline ensured that no one shouted out. The centurion said, *"Right, we'll start with you, Marcellus. Rufus, you, Hermes, Timon, and you too Jonam. Fall out and line up next to Marcellus. Carry on."*

The leather thongs with bits of bone and metal tied to the ends whistled though the air and tore into the flesh of Yeshua's back.

Crack! Gasp
Crack! Gasp
Crack! Gasp
Crack! Gasp

Blood began trickling down Yeshua's body. His face was set, his teeth clenched.

Crack! Gasp
Crack! Gasp
Crack! Gasp
Crack! Gasp

"Well done, Marcellus. Neat work. Rufus, you take over."

And so on...

COMMENT

1 Why was Jesus scourged?

Mark puts the scourging of Jesus as part of the punishment of crucifixion, which seems to have been normal practice. John puts it as an attempt by Pilate to deal with Jesus by the lesser punishment, just as the Albinus was to do thirty years later. Albinus was procurator of Judaea and Samaria in 62 CE. The chief priests wanted to get rid of a popular speaker who was constantly attacking the Temple and the priests. They arrested him and handed him over to the procurator, asking for him to be crucified as a disturber of the peace. Albinus interviewed him and ignored the Temple authorities. Instead he had the troublemaker scourged and then released him as a madman.

It was only when scourging Jesus failed to placate the crowd and the chief priests that Pilate ordered the crucifixion. 'Jesus the Troublemaker' follows Mark, but the procedure of carrying out the scourging would have been the same in both cases. The only thing we can say with certainty is that Jesus was not flogged twice - he could well have died from it before he was fixed to the cross.

2 How many soldiers?

The NRSV says that the whole cohort was there, meaning 480 soldiers. But the word in Greek does not necessarily mean cohort. The NIV uses 'company'. The New King James Version has 'garrison'. The Authorised Version of 1611 has the correct translation of 'band'. The word in Greek is 'speira' which is quite indeterminate. It is used in John 18.3 for the detachment of soldiers sent to arrest Jesus. So how many soldiers were there? We do not know. It could have been a third of a cohort, i.e. 125 men, or a squad of ten under their decurion. I chose the basic Roman military unit of a hundred soldiers under a centurion.

3 How bad was a Roman scourging?

The Roman historian Livy mentions twice that after being *'beaten with lashes (the prisoners) were fastened to the cross.'* (M Hengel, Cucifixion). Seneca describes the process of crucifixion and includes the detail of *'swelling with ugly weals on shoulders and chest'*, presumably from being scourged.

The instrument used in scourging was a 'flagellum' or 'flagrum' made up of leather thongs with lead tips at the ends. If the Turin shroud is authentic, then it seems that Jesus was flogged with a flagrum consisting of three separate thongs, ending with one or two lead balls. It is no wonder that it was not uncommon for men to die from shock and blood loss as a consequence of the flogging.

4 The soldiers' mockery

Both Mark and John report that the soldiers engaged in ridiculing Jesus, dressing him up as a pretend king in a purple cloak and a crown of thorns. Luke places this at the end of the interrogation by Herod Antipas. It was not meant to inflict more pain, just a mob reaction to a vulnerable person. Canteen culture at work. And for them to call Jesus 'King of the Jews' was just another form of mockery, as I believe was Pilate's placard, detailing Jesus' 'crime' at the head of the cross.

REFLECTION

Scourging was a standard punishment throughout human history, carried out by Jews, Romans and the British Navy. Paul records: *"Five times I received from the Jews the forty lashes minus one. Three times I was beaten with rods. Once I received a stoning.'* (2 Corinthians 11.24-25). It was meant to inflict pain and ensure obedience. This it failed to do so fairly spectacularly in Paul's case, as it does today with countless Christians who suffer imprisonment and torture in today's totalitarian states.

It was not just the physical pain. I remember when I was young disagreeing profoundly with the schoolboy saying, *'Sticks and stones may break my bones but words can never hurt me'*. Both hurt. Mockery is hard to take. It can make us doubt ourselves and everything we have worked for.

Less than twelve hours earlier, Jesus had finally prayed, *"Father, your will be done."* Was he able to turn even this mocking into prayer? Richard Wurmbrand spent three years in solitary confinement under the Rumanian Communist regime. In his sermons to himself he said, *"Let it be enough for you that you are suffering for the Kingdom of God. All suffering serves this final cause."*

    (Sermons in Solitary Confinement/Alone with God p. 61)

SUGGESTION

Many Christians in the first three centuries endured barbaric tortures and deaths, such as Polycarp, Perpetua and Felicity or the martyrs of Lyons. Look them up on the internet; there is a 'List of Christian Martyrs' on Wikipedia. Spend some time praying for Christians being persecuted today.

MONDAY OF HOLY WEEK – WALK TO GETHSEMANE

The soldiers led Jesus out to crucify him. They compelled a passer-by, who was coming in from the country, to carry his cross; it was Simon of Cyrene, the father of Alexander and Rufus. Then they brought Jesus to the place called Golgotha (which means the place of a skull). And they offered him wine mixed with myrrh; but he did not take it. And they crucified him, and divided his clothes among them, casting lots to decide what each should take.

(Mark 15.20-24)

THE SCENE

The ten man squad loaded the heavy cross beams on to the shoulders of each of the prisoners, two of them fluently cursing Rome, the soldiers and their fate. All three prisoners were made to walk across the mosaic pavement, down the steps to the main gate and out to the street opposite the City Market. Yeshua staggered and almost fell going down the stone steps. A soldier put his hand out to steady the cross beam. They turned left on to Market Street where a crowd of the curious had gathered. They quickly recognised Yeshua, because he was the only one wearing a tunic and cloak, and the wreath of thorns was still on his head. Jeers and catcalls greeted Yeshua, and some rotten fruit, until the soldiers made a threatening move towards the crowd and stopped it. A couple of hundred yards further, the party came to the Hippichus Gate, which Yeshua had walked through freely only half a day before. Just before reaching it, the weight of the crossbeam proved too much for him, and Yeshua collapsed on the flagstones.

One of the older soldiers scanned the pedestrians entering through the gate and seized on a young man wearing a merchant's cloak and with an African-type face.

"Here, you, carry this crossbeam."

"It's got nothing to do with me. I don't even live here."

"I don't care. You're going to do it, and we're going to have no delay. Just up to that hillock outside the gate. Right?"

The young man with a Berber complexion looked ready to explode with resentment, but then he looked at the prisoner, whose expression of total acceptance, whatever happened, took the wind out of his sails.

"All right, come on, let's have it. If it'll help you, mate. Not because of these pigs."

He loaded the crossbeam on his shoulders and Yeshua followed him, at last able to walk upright. They walked along the path which skirted the city wall until they were opposite a small rocky hill, with its half dozen wooden uprights ready today to become the instruments of agonising death for three men. Skull Hill.

COMMENT

1 Stations of the Cross

The stations of the cross originated in the Via Sacra, or Via Dolorosa, in Jerusalem, which pilgrims would walk along as an act of devotion. By the 16th century fourteen stations were described in a German book 'Geystlich Strass' (Spiritual Road). The stations were originally always set up in the open air, but in 1686 the Pope allowed Franciscan friars to set them up inside their churches. This permission was extended to all Catholic churches in 1731. They are now in all Catholic Churches and in half Anglican ones.

The story they tell is much more complex than the simple account in the gospels. Jesus meeting his mother, then Veronica, and falling three times are all later additions to the original account. They are not included in the Stations of the Cross used in the Philippines, which stay much closer to the gospels. And the actual route of the Via Dolorosa in Jerusalem does not follow the street plan of 1st century Jerusalem.

2 The Women

Luke's gospel relates one incident which is picked up by the Stations of the Cross - the grieving women who accompanied Jesus on his final walk.

A great number of the people followed him, and among them were women who were beating their breasts and wailing for him. But Jesus turned to them and said, 'Daughters of Jerusalem, do not weep for me, but weep for yourselves and for your children. For the days are surely coming when they will say, "Blessed are the barren, and the wombs that never bore, and the breasts that never nursed." Then they will begin to say to the mountains, "Fall on us"; and to the hills, "Cover us." For if they do this when the wood is green, what will happen when it is dry?'

(Luke 23.27-31)

Luke tells us three things through this:

A lot of people followed the execution party. This is likely. When an accident happens on the motorway, traffic always slows while drivers take a look.

Some women, inhabitants of Jerusalem, came to grieve at the awful fate awaiting the prophet from Galilee. I guess they would have come from the Lower City, where the poorer inhabitants lived. Apparently they were not Galilean pilgrims. Were they the majority or the minority of the crowd?. We don't know.

Jesus spoke to them - quite a lengthy speech. It is possible that he may have said something simpler like: *"Daughters of Jerusalem, do not weep for me, but weep for yourselves and for your children. If they do this when the wood is green, what will happen when it is dry?'* Luke may have expanded this by incorporating the prophecies of Mark 13.17 and Hosea 10.8). In the ancient world it was normal to create speeches which are like what the person would have said.

3 The route
The Via Dolorosa assumes that the starting point was the Ecce Homo Convent, near St Stephen's Gate/ Lion Gate. The actual route that Jesus took would have been from the Roman barracks in Herod's palace, next to Jaffa gate, to the hill of Golgotha, within the Church of the Holy Sepulchre (or Church of the Resurrection). The distance is 350 metres or 1,000 feet. Today you would take the Greek Catholic Patriarchate Road and wind your way there in no more than fifteen minutes. The traditional Via Dolorosa is three times that distance.

4 Simon of Cyrene
Mark clearly knew two members of the church, Alexander and Rufus. *"Our father actually helped Jesus carry his cross!"*. They were clearly Jewish Christians despite their Greek names as Simon is a Jewish name - Shim'on. A real confirmation of the historical worth of Marks' gospel.

Cyrene was a major city in what is now Libya. It was built on a rocky outpost ten miles from its port. There was a large Jewish population, which had increasingly fraught relations with the more numerous Greek inhabitants. Its chief export was a specific plant used as contraceptive. There was a very bloody Jewish revolt in 73 and again in 115. It was finally ruined by an earthquake in 262 AD.

5 The Cross

Jesus is normally portrayed as carrying a complete cross, both the upright and the cross beam. In fact the upright stake would already have been fixed in the ground. Jesus carried the crossbeam - a weighty piece of work as it had to support the entire weight of his body. Zeffirelli's series 'Jesus of Nazareth' has a convincing reconstruction of a wooden framework to which the cross piece was attached. I guessed that it was not attached by nails, but that a metal scoop was attached to the upright into which the crossbeam was dropped. Just an idea.

REFLECTION

1 Jesus was suffering intense pain and exhaustion, knowing that nothing lay ahead in the near future than more pain and more exhaustion. He also had had to face the unrelenting hostility of his fellow Jews and the dismissive incomprehension of the Gentile military. In the midst of it all, a ray of light. The officer in charge realised that Jesus might not make it the couple of hundred yards to the execution site. Either because he did not want to make Jesus' punishment still more brutal, or because he did not want the prisoner's weakness to hold up the proceedings, he drafted in a stranger to carry the crossbeam. Whichever it was, he simply carried out his orders without adding to Jesus' suffering.

Jesus spoke of this in the Sermon on the Mount: *"If anyone forces you to go one mile, go also the second mile"*. (Matthew 5.41). It refers to the Roman practice in which a soldier could require a civilian to carry his pack for one mile. Jesus here teaches his followers literally to go the extra mile. To turn a forced obedience into a voluntary action, and so reset the relationship.

2 I doubt that the order to carry Jesus' crossbeam reset Simon's relationship with the occupation troops. Most likely he had come from North Africa to attend the Passover celebrations in the Temple, and was camping outside the walls. Carrying a criminal's cross was the last thing he wanted to do. But it seems that the encounter had a transformative effect. He and his family became part of the Jesus movement for the next thirty years. All because he was willing to help a condemned prisoner.

There is an echo in the life of St Martin of Tours, a Roman soldier about twenty years old. In 336 he was taking instruction before making the life-changing decision of being baptised as a Christian. One cold winter's day he saw a destitute beggar outside the gate of Amiens, shivering with cold. He had no spare clothing, so he cut his military cloak in half and gave half of it to the beggar. That night he had a dream in which he saw Jesus wearing the half cloak Martin had given to the beggar. Immediately he requested baptism and resigned from the army - before he had finally become a Christian.

3 There are two dimensions to this story: helping and being helped.

There is a blessing to helping. Paul gives us an otherwise unknown saying of Jesus, quoted by Luke: *'It is more blessed to give than to receive.'* (Acts 20.35)

And there is a blessing to being helped. Not just being assisted in something we cannot otherwise do. Simply accepting help. Often this is hard to do. Especially when we feel under pressure and an offer to help can seem an intrusion into our panicky concentration on the task in hand. Sometimes we need to stop, take a breath and accept the proffered help. And say thank you. Often relationships are built and nurtured not so much by helping as by accepting help.

SUGGESTION

Think about an instance in the last few days where you have been able to help someone, and when you have accepted help. Thank God for both.

TUESDAY OF HOLY WEEK – THE KINDNESS AND UNKINDNESS OF STRANGERS

*T*hen the soldiers brought Jesus to the place called Golgotha *(which means the place of a skull). And they offered him wine mixed with myrrh; but he did not take it.*

And they crucified him, and divided his clothes among them, casting lots to decide what each should take. It was nine o'clock in the morning when they crucified him. The inscription of the charge against him read, 'The King of the Jews.' And with him they crucified two bandits, one on his right and one on his left.

Those who passed by derided him, shaking their heads and saying, 'Aha! You who would destroy the temple and build it in three days, save yourself, and come down from the cross!' In the same way the chief priests, along with the scribes, were also mocking him among themselves and saying, 'He saved others; he cannot save himself. Let the Messiah, the King of Israel, come down from the cross now, so that we may see and believe.' Those who were crucified with him also taunted him.

(Mark 15.22-32)

THE SCENE

As the party climbed the rocky knoll, three bugle calls were heard faintly from the Antonia, marking the start of the morning watch. As they reached the top, a couple of elderly women offered each of the prisoners a drink from a jug they had with them - wine mixed with myrrh to deaden the pain. The two robbers drank greedily. Yeshua took one drink, then turned his head away.

A crowd of onlookers stood on the path by the city wall, less than fifty yards from the gruesome sight. Some

259

were only too happy to see Yeshua suffering there.

"Hey, prophet, you still going to destroy the Temple and rebuild it in three days?"

"You going to get off the cross and stop me trading in the Temple again? I don't think so!"

One of the soldiers stretched himself and looked carefully at the 'titulus'.

"King of the Jews, eh? Person of power? Not very powerful now, are you?"

He laughed nastily.

COMMENT

1 Wine and Myrrh

Myrrh was widely used in Roman times to reduce pain. We do not know who gave Jesus the pain-deadening drink. It is unlikely to have been the soldiers. Roman solders on crucifixion duty often actually increased the condemned men's pain by various imaginative tortures such as twisting the body or nailing the genitals. Jewish tradition is that a mixture of wine and myrrh was given out to condemned prisoners by charitable women, following the description of one such in Proverbs 31.6-7:

Give strong drink to one who is perishing,
*   and wine to those in bitter distress;*
let them drink and forget their poverty,
*   and remember their misery no more.*

2 'The King of the Jews'

The placard or 'titulus' fixed over the head of Jesus detailing his crime was 'the King of the Jews' in Hebrew, Latin, and Greek. This was not a covert statement of faith by Pilate. After all, his soldiers used the phrase to extract maximum fun from their cruel horseplay after the scourging. Rather, it was a calculated insult to both Jesus and the Jewish authorities. It would be like executing Patrick Pearse, one of the leaders of the Easter Rising in Dublin in 1915, with a placard round his neck saying 'President of Ireland'.

3 The taunts of the crowd

Mark records the crowd as mocking Jesus' claim that after the Temple was destroyed, he would raise it in three days. The chief priests and scribes mocked his claim to be the Messiah. Both of these taunts came from the early morning trial in Caiaphas' palace. In other words, it was people from the palace who made up the crowd, not the general population. Rubbing salt into the wound.

REFLECTION

1 Not drinking the wine

This is the last independent action that Jesus took. In a few moments his hands and feet would be permanently nailed to the cross. It was a conscious decision. He did not touch the wine with its mixture of myrrh. Myrrh was a common analgesic in the ancient world, used to deaden pain. Later on he did accept wine from a soldier. So it was the the myrrh which made him refuse it. He wanted nothing to blunt his consciousness, even of the coming torment. He would face the excruciating agony of a slow death on the cross fully conscious and so able to offer it to God. Such courage is almost inconceivable.

2 King?

When Pilate asked Jesus, "Are you the King of the Jews?" Jesus did not deny it. "It's as you say." But the title 'King' sits uneasily on Jesus. Nowhere in Mark, Luke and John does Jesus refer himself in any way as a king. In his account of the feeding of the five thousand, John writes, *'when Jesus realised that they were about to come and take him by force to make him king, he withdrew again to the mountain by himself.'* (6.15). Only Matthew refers to Jesus as king, in the parable of the wedding banquet (22.1-14) and the sheep and the goats (25.31-46). Both these seem to be developments by the early church, wanting to magnify the authority and status of the risen Jesus. How do we see Jesus? As a great authority figure? Or, in the words of the prayer from St Richard of Chichester, 'my redeemer, friend and brother'?

3 Losing reputation

The mockery of the crowd sealed the loss of all of Jesus' public reputation. Even his disciples, after the crucifixion, referred to him in the past tense, *"we had hoped that he was the one to redeem Israel."* (Luke 24.21) Loss of reputation makes one an outcast. How could we live with ourselves or others if our reputation was destroyed?

SUGGESTION

Pray the prayer ascribed to St Richard of Chichester (1197 -m1253)

Thanks be to you, O Lord Jesus Christ,
for all the benefits you have given to me,
   for all the pains and insults you have borne for me.
  O most merciful Redeemer, Friend and Bother,
  may I know you more clearly,
  love you more dearly,

and follow you more nearly
day by day.

The last five lines were added in the early 20th century.
Whoever did so deserves the thanks of the whole
Christian community.

WEDNESDAY OF HOLY WEEK – FATHER, FORGIVE

When they came to the place that is called The Skull, they crucified Jesus there with the criminals, one on his right and one on his left. Then Jesus said, 'Father, forgive them; for they do not know what they are doing.'

(Luke 23.33-34)

THE SCENE

Each squad of four soldiers took their prisoner, stretched them out on the ground and hammered a heavy nail into each wrist-joint. The two robbers shrieked in agony. Yeshua clenched his jaw convulsively, but at each hammer blow prayed aloud, *"Abba forgive."*

Bang

"Abba forgive."

Bang

"Abba forgive."

Bang

"Abba forgive."

Bang

"Abba forgive."

Bang

"Abba forgive."

Bang

"Abba forgive. They don't know - what - they're doing."

COMMENT

1 The nailing

In my account of the crucifixion I assume that three hammer blows were needed to drive each of the large nails through the wrists. The feet came later. I also assume that Jesus' prayer was short as it was said through gritted teeth.

He also would have used his favourite word for father, the intimate 'Abba'.

2 Did it happen?

The earliest copy of Luke's gospel, which comes from around 250 AD, does not include the saying about forgiveness, nor do four major texts from the fourth and fifth centuries. It is included in two major texts from the fifth century, but it is quoted by four major theologians of the second and third centuries. Was it a free-floating piece of oral tradition that found its home in this passage in Luke?

Jesus' words of forgiveness are certainly of a piece with his teaching about forgiveness, and its reproduction in the death of Stephen, the first Christian martyr, who died crying out, *"Lord, do not hold this sin against them."* (Acts 7.60) *"Father forgive them"* are not just words which Jesus spoke. They are who he is.

3 Forgiving whom?

When Jesus said, "Father forgive them, they do not know what they are doing," did he mean the soldiers hammering nails into his hands and feet; or all those involved in his execution including Caiaphas and Pilate? I think he meant the squaddies directly in front of him. But does it matter? All of us are ignorant of what we are ultimately doing.

REFLECTION

1 Coventry

On the night of 14th November 1940 a total of 515 German bombers dropped over 500 tonnes of high explosives on Coventry, devastating the city centre and creating a firestorm. 568 people were killed and 4,000 homes were destroyed. The cathedral was set on fire and all the interior destroyed. The next day Goebbels, the Nazi propaganda minister coined a new word: 'coventrieren'.

In the morning Provost Richard Howard, standing in the smouldering ruins, made the decision to rebuild the cathedral. He had the words 'Father Forgive' inscribed on the wall at the east end. The stonemason Jack Forbes found two charred timbers fallen in the shape of the cross, lashed them together and set them up on the altar ruins. Three of the medieval nails were formed into a cross, and after the war one was given to the Kaiser Wilhelm Memorial Church in Berlin, also destroyed by bombing. The cathedral became a centre for international reconciliation, with especially close links to the church in Dresden, East Germany.

Coventry Cathedral teaches us a great deal about forgiveness. It is not a one-off event it is a journey. The journey starts with the decision to face forward rather than back, and to abandon thoughts of bitterness, hatred and revenge. As I heard the Dalai Lama say, *"Anger is sometimes useful. Hatred never is."* The next step is to take action. This may mean rebuilding a cathedral. It may mean rebuilding one's life.

2 Singapore

Leonard Wilson became bishop of Singapore in 1941. In 1942 Singapore fell to the Japanese, and in 1943 Bishop Leonard was interned in Changi prison camp. There he was tortured, with Japanese soldiers taking turns in flaying his back with rods while he was strapped to a table. (I heard him describe his experiences in a sermon I heard as a teenager). He found it a struggle to forgive his tormentors. He imagined them as children, and it is hard to hate children. But ultimately he was able to forgive them by imagining what they would be like if they became Christians. Later, he did meet one of his torturers who had come to faith, and indeed, the change in him was unmistakable.

SUGGESTION

Think of something in your life where you have been forgiven or been able to forgive. What were the results? How do you feel about it now?

THURSDAY OF HOLY WEEK, MAUNDY THURSDAY – MARY AND JOHN

Standing near the cross of Jesus were his mother, and his mother's sister, Mary the wife of Clopas, and Mary Magdalene. When Jesus saw his mother and the disciple whom he loved standing beside her, he said to his mother, 'Woman, here is your son.' Then he said to the disciple, 'Here is your mother.' And from that hour the disciple took her into his own home.

(John 19.25-27)

THE SCENE

"'Ere, what' happening? Gone a bit dark. P'raps we should have brought some lanterns. Weird." The soldiers started to feel nervous, but were definitely not going to show their comrades that they were scared.

Pain.

Pain.

Pain.

Darkness.

A group of half a dozen women arrived on the path, keening a lament and sobbing uncontrollably. Yeshua raised his head and searched the group. He tried to say something. An elderly woman and a young man came as close as the soldiers would allow. With every breath an effort, Yeshua said,

"Mother - your son - Son - your mother." The young man bowed his head in understanding, put his arm around the woman and led her away weeping.

Pain.

COMMENT

1 Crucifixion

Jesus' words to his mother and beloved disciple did not come out of a vacuum. They came out of a setting of extreme pain. The Stoic philosopher Seneca the Younger (4 BCE - 65 CE) described the experience of being crucified:

'Can anyone be found who would prefer wasting away in pain, dying limb by limb, or letting out his life drop by drop, rather than expiring once for all? Can any man be found willing to be fastened to the accursed tree, long sickly, already deformed, swelling with ugly weals on shoulders and chest, and drawing the breath of life amid long-drawn-out agony? He would have many excuses for dying even before mounting the cross.'

(from Martin Hengel, 'Crucifixion')

This is why in my account Jesus is able only to gasp out single words, not complete sentences.

2 The Women

John tells us of four women at the cross, (assuming that Mary's sister was not also called Mary): Jesus' mother, his aunt, the wife of Clopas and Mary from Magdala.

Mark says there were a number of women, including Mary from Magdala, Salome and the mother of James and Joseph, but not Jesus' mother. Perhaps Mary is not in this list because after the words of Jesus, the beloved disciple led her away.

Luke just says that his acquaintances, including the women who had followed him from Galilee, watched from a distance.

3 The beloved disciple?

Who was this disciple whom Jesus loved, who took Mary, mother of Jesus, under his wing? Traditionally it was the writer of the Gospel of John. That does make sense. Otherwise why should this one disciple be unnamed?

But he is not unnamed in early church tradition. He is John, John son of Zebedee, or Yochanan Bar-Zavdai, brother of James, or in Hebrew, Yacoub. Yet it does seem strange that virtually all of the gospel takes place in Jerusalem. Apart from chapter 6 and the appendix in chapter 21, only 22 verses take place in Galilee.

In 'The Testimony of the Beloved Disciple' Richard Baukham argues that the writer of the gospel was a Jerusalem disciple called John. There was an early tradition that in Ephesus there were tombs where two Johns were buried who had seen the Lord. And we do know of another Jerusalem 'disciple whom Jesus loved' - Lazarus of Bethany.

4 A refuge for Mary

It makes sense that Jesus should entrust his mother to a Jerusalem disciple, who could indeed take her into his own home 'at that hour'. It was perhaps the same house where Jesus held the Last Supper. He was not entrusting her to a disciple who lived five days' walk away in Galilee. And Jesus was not breaking up his family. Luke tells us in Acts 1.14 that six weeks later the 120 disciples who met regularly for prayer included 'Mary the mother of Jesus, as well as his brothers' - Yacoub, Yosef, Y'hudah and Shim'on (Mark 6.3)

5 Maundy Thursday

Maundy Thursday is the name given to the day before Good Friday when the Church recalls the Last Supper. The word 'Maundy' is a corruption of the Latin 'Mandatum' or 'commandment'. It is taken from John's account of the Last Supper, John 13.34: *'I give you a new commandment, that you love one another. Just as I have loved you, you also should love one another.'*

REFLECTION

1 New family

In the midst of all his suffering, physical, mental, spiritual, Jesus found the strength to care for those closest to him. Not only does he give his mother a place of refuge, but also a new relationship on which she can depend. Jesus also unites his Jerusalem follower with his Galilean family connections. From now on the new Jesus movement, 'the Way' (Acts 9.2), will be led by Galilean disciples and centred in Jerusalem.

2 Suffering and selfishness

Suffering almost inevitably makes us selfish. Pain and discomfort cry out for relief. If someone is nearby, we want them to step up to the plate and do something. We can all too easily see the other person primarily through the lens of our own suffering. Suffering can create in us a sense of entitlement, and this can drive away help rather than produce it.

If anyone had an excuse to let himself be engulfed by his suffering, it was Jesus on the cross. But in today's passage we see him looking beyond himself to the needs of others, the needs of those standing directly in front of him.

Let's be patient, with ourselves as well as with others. I used to have a lapel badge with the letters: PBPWM - GHNFWMY. It stands for: Please be Patient With Me - God Has Not Finished With Me Yet.

SUGGESTION

Pray for this closest to us, those who see us at our best and at our worst. Thank God for them, and teach us how to serve each other better.

Here is a useful prayer taken from Alcoholics Anonymous (p.83)

'Please show me the way of patience, tolerance, kindness and love.'

GOOD FRIDAY - FORSAKEN

When it was noon, darkness came over the whole land until three in the afternoon. At three o'clock Jesus cried out with a loud voice, 'Eloi, Eloi, lema sabachthani?' which means, 'My God, my God, why have you forsaken me?' When some of the bystanders heard it, they said, 'Listen, he is calling for Elijah.' And someone ran, filled a sponge with sour wine, put it on a stick, and gave it to him to drink, saying, 'Wait, let us see whether Elijah will come to take him down.' Then Jesus gave a loud cry and breathed his last.

(Mark 15.33-37)

THE SCENE

Pain.

Darkness.

Yeshua made a supreme effort, raised himself on his tortured feet, took a deep breath and made the terrible cry,

"Elohi! Elohi! L'mah sh'vaktani?"
"'Ere, sound like 'e's calling for Prophet Elijah."
"Well, you'd know, you're one of them."
"Maybe he's thirsty."
"Oh yeah, he'll be thirsty all right."
"Look, I'm going to give him some of our plonk. Anyone got a sponge? Ta. A stick or a javelin? That's great. 'Ere you are, mate."
"Nah, stop it, let's see if this Elijah fellow will come down and take him away."
"Go on, get away, I'll just give him a drink."

Yeshua's whole body suddenly stiffened, his face lifted up to the sky, as he gave a last shout.
"It's done!"
His body collapsed down again, his head dropped to his chest. His lips moved for a few moments and then ceased. His chest was still.

Dead.

COMMENT

1 Mark and Matthew are the only two gospels to record Jesus' cry of agony, *"My God, my God, why have you forsaken me?"* It is inconceivable that such a cry of despair could have been invented.

It is a quote of the opening line of Psalm 22, which continues the theme of lament for the next twenty verses, only moving to praise in the last ten.

Mark does not tell us if Jesus' last shout was made up of words or not. If it was, *"It is finished"* (John 19.30) seems more likely than the whole sentence *"Father, into your hands I commend my spirit."* (Luke 23.46)

2 The soldiers' offer of 'sour wine' - the ordinary rough wine of the common people - seems to have been a simple act of compassion or curiosity. They were not trying to make Jesus' suffering worse.

3 Jesus seems to have died more quickly than normal, both because he had been weakened by the scourging, and by his choice of remaining fully conscious of the pain.

REFLECTION

Here we stand on holy ground. Jesus' use of Psalm 22 invites us to participate in his final struggle with God - the God who often seems to absent himself when we need him most. What must it have been like for Jesus, who had spent his life in intimate relationship with God his Father, to have all consciousness of that relationship to be taken away in the hour of his greatest need? The only response we can have is to sit in silence - anything else is too trivial. Silence and contemplation of the cross.

And yet - perhaps there is something to say.

Was Jesus' cry of despair his final recognition that the universe is meaningless? Or was it the moment of his final identification with the whole of suffering creation?. Perhaps this was the moment when the Father, through Jesus, took within himself every physical, mental and spiritual darkness with which men and women are plagued. We don't know. But perhaps this poem by the First World War chaplain, Student Kennedy, is appropriate.

HE WAS A GAMBLER TOO
And sitting down they watched him there,
The soldiers did.
There, while they played with dice
He made his sacrifice
And died upon the cross
To rid the world of sin

He was a gambler too, my Christ.
He took his life and threw it for a world redeemed.
And ere the westering sun went down,
Crowning the day with its crimson crown,
He knew that he had won.

SUGGESTION

Stand in front of an image of Jesus on the cross, or simply stand at a window, looking out on to the world, and read aloud Psalm 22.

HOLY SATURDAY - SAD SABBATH

*T*hen *Jesus gave a loud cry and breathed his last. And the
curtain of the temple was torn in two, from top to bottom.
Now when the centurion, who stood facing him, saw that in this
way he breathed his last, he said, 'Truly this man was God's Son!'*

*When evening had come, and since it was the day of Preparation,
that is, the day before the sabbath, Joseph of Arimathea, a
respected member of the council, who was also himself waiting
expectantly for the kingdom of God, went boldly to Pilate and
asked for the body of Jesus. Then Pilate wondered if he were
already dead; and summoning the centurion, he asked him
whether he had been dead for some time. When he learned from
the centurion that he was dead, he granted the body to Joseph.
Then Joseph bought a linen cloth, and taking down the body,
wrapped it in the linen cloth, and laid it in a tomb that had been
hewn out of the rock. He then rolled a stone against the door of the
tomb. Mary Magdalene and Mary the mother of Joses saw where
the body was laid.*

(Mark 15.38-38, 42-47)

THE SCENE

An imaginary conversation between Caiaphas and his wife
in their bedroom.

> "When we took him to Pilatus, the procurator started being
> very officious, asking tricky questions and in the end sending
> him over to Herod Antipas."

> "You've never been a patient man, Yosef, you must have been
> going out of your mind!"

> "Rather. Especially as Herod didn't really want to be
> bothered and sent him back to Pilatus."

"So that started all over again?'

"In a way. Our friend Pontius took him inside and questioned him privately. But that gave us the opportunity to arrange a large, excitable and local Jerusalem crowd to see that we finally got shot of him. With a bit of encouragement, the crowd went wild asking for Yeshua's crucifixion, and Pilatus, never a man of principle, caved in. So by mid-morning our man was nailed up to a wooden crosspiece and died some hours later. And not a whiff of violence from his so-called supporters."

"What a relief. But I can see why you're so stressed. Shall I call my maid in to give you a nice back massage?"

"Perhaps in a while. But let me finish the story first."

"There's more?

"A little. I had to go to the Temple to officiate at the sacrifices. Mid-afternoon, we got the news of his death, and just then the great curtain separating the Holy Place from the Holy of Holies tore itself in two, from top to bottom!"

"No! How dreadful? Who could have done that?"

"It's a total mystery. No one knows. Maybe this Yeshua was actually a wizard who had learnt his spells in Egypt. Anyway, it shook us all. And then I heard that my namesake, Yosef Ramatayim from the Council, had gone over my head, and had appealed directly to Pilatus to have the body given to him for burial. He should have been thrown in the lime pit with the other two low-lifes."

"I've never liked him. Too priggish by far."

"He is. One of those annoying bleeding hearts. Anyway, their dead prophet is now lying in a rock tomb at the foot of Skull Hill. No wonder it hadn't been used. No one wants to be buried there!"

"Well, dear, come to bed. You've certainly heard the last of this troublemaker."

COMMENT

1 The Centurion

The centurion, equivalent to a sergeant-major, was impressed by Jesus. In Luke he says, *"Certainly this man was innocent."* (Luke 23.47). In Mark he says, *"Truly this man was God's Son!"* (Mark 15.39). He did not say, *"This man was the Son of God."* His words were rather, *"This man was a son of God"*, - or as I think more likely, *"This man was a son of the gods."* In other words he was recognising Jesus' essential goodness rather than making a declaration of faith.

2 The Temple Curtain

An impressive treasure of the Temple was the enormous curtain, sixty foot high, which separated the Holy Place from the Holy of Holies. Josephus described it in 'the Jewish War': *'It was of Babylonian tapestry, with embroidery of blue and fine linen, of scarlet also and purple, wrought with marvellous skill. Nor was this mixture of materials without its mystic meaning: it typified the universe.'* It was eventually taken to Rome after the destruction of the Temple in 70 AD.

Mark and Luke both say that when Jesus died, *'the curtain of the temple was torn in two, from top to bottom'.* It does not occur in John. There is no independent witness to the tearing of the curtain.

What would it have meant? To Christian eyes, it was an object lesson that the religious rules that separated people from God had now been done away with. The Letter to the Hebrews makes this point: *'Since we have confidence to enter the sanctuary by the blood of Jesus, by the new and living way that he opened for us through the curtain (that is, through his flesh), and since we have a great priest over the house of God, let us approach with a true heart in full assurance of faith, with our hearts sprinkled clean from an evil conscience and our bodies washed with pure water.'* (Hebrew 10.19-22)

To Jewish eyes, it might have seemed like a prophecy of the coming destruction of the Temple; or possibly, as in my imaginary conversation between Caiaphas and his wife, and as the writers of the Talmud might have believed, an act of wizardry.

3 The Burial
'I handed on to you as of first importance what I in turn had received: that Christ died for our sins in accordance with the scriptures, and that he was buried ...'

(1 Corinthians 15.3-4)

Paul's emphasis on the burial of Jesus is interesting. It is his way of emphasising that Jesus had a real physical human body. He was not just a spiritual being.

The gospels are all equally explicit about the burial. It was clearly a rush job because it had to be finished before sunset when the sabbath began. (Incidentally, all four gospels agree that the crucifixion happened on the Day of Preparation before the sabbath). John says that Joseph of Arimathea was joined by Nicodemus who brought an enormous quantity of spices with him. I can't see this myself. I think that, as Mark describes, it was a rush job and Jesus' women followers had to buy spices during the following evening to give Jesus' body the proper anointing.

4 The Church of the Holy Sepulchre

Burial was different in the rocky landscape of Judaea. It was not being put in a hole in the ground. The body would be placed ceremoniously in a small cave and a large millstone rolled along a groove with a bump at the end to block the entrance. When Constantine became a Christian, the traditional site of the crucifixion and burial of Jesus were placed in an open plaza within the church, and the unnecessary rock cut away. In 1009 when Caliph Al-Hakim destroyed the church of the Holy Sepulchre, he had the cave and its rocky surrounds chiselled away. The present site of the Holy Sepulchre is a later construction. But just behind the Syrian Orthodox chapel at the eastern end is a series of other rock tombs. The whole area of the rocky knoll and the caves at the base was simply a place of death.

REFLECTION

Our attitude to death

A number of years ago the London magazine Time Out carried an interview with the British film director Nicholas Roeg, ('Performance', 'Don't Look Now'). In it the interviewer asked why so many of his films ended in tragedy. Roeg replied, *"Well, I don't regard death as a tragedy. If it is, we are all in deep shit."*

Daniel Craig's final film as 007, 'No Time to Die', ends with M reading from a book, (Ian Fleming's quotation from Jack London in 'You only Live twice', slightly altered). *"The proper function of man is to live, not to exist. I shall use my time. I shall not waste my days in trying to prolong them."*

I saw the film with a friend of mine, a lady of a certain age, like myself. We both agreed absolutely with the sentiment.

I once took a fortnight's course in counselling. My main memory of it is the sentence, *"Children will not fear life if their parents have the courage not to fear death".*

It is put even better by the 17th century poet John Donne:

> Death, be not proud, though some have called thee
> Mighty and dreadful, for thou art not so;
> For those whom thou think'st thou dost overthrow
> Die not, poor Death, nor yet canst thou kill me.
> From rest and sleep, which but thy pictures be,
> Much pleasure; then from thee much more must flow,
> And soonest our best men with thee do go,
> Rest of their bones, and soul's delivery.
> Thou art slave to fate, chance, kings, and desperate men,
> And dost with poison, war, and sickness dwell,
> And poppy or charms can make us sleep as well
> And better than thy stroke; why swell'st thou then?
> One short sleep past, we wake eternally
> And death shall be no more; Death, thou shalt die.

SUGGESTION

Perhaps the finest hymn about Holy Week is 'My song is love unknown', written by the clergyman Samuel Crossman in 1664. It is often sung in church, but the verse about Jesus' burial is usually omitted. Because the church does not much like looking into the shadows? But they are there. Here is the verse.

> *In life, no house, no home*
> *My Lord on earth might have;*
> *In death no friendly tomb*
> *But what a stranger gave.*
> *What may I say? Heav'n was His home;*
> *But mine the tomb wherein He lay.*

You can find the whole hymn on YouTube.

EASTER

THE EMPTY TOMB

Jewish tomb near Megiddo

EASTER DAY - RESURRECTION!

When the sabbath was over, Mary Magdalene, and Mary the mother of James, and Salome bought spices, so that they might go and anoint him. And very early on the first day of the week, when the sun had risen, they went to the tomb. They had been saying to one another, 'Who will roll away the stone for us from the entrance to the tomb?' When they looked up, they saw that the stone, which was very large, had already been rolled back. As they entered the tomb, they saw a young man, dressed in a white robe, sitting on the right side; and they were alarmed. But he said to them, 'Do not be alarmed; you are looking for Jesus of Nazareth, who was crucified. He has been raised; he is not here. Look, there is the place they laid him. But go, tell his disciples and Peter that he is going ahead of you to Galilee; there you will see him, just as he told you.' So they went out and fled from the tomb, for terror and amazement had seized them; and they said nothing to anyone, for they were afraid.

(Mark 16.1-8)

Early on the first day of the week, while it was still dark, Mary Magdalene came to the tomb and saw that the stone had been removed from the tomb. So she ran and went to Simon Peter and the other disciple, the one whom Jesus loved, and said to them, 'They have taken the Lord out of the tomb, and we do not know where they have laid him.' Then Peter and the other disciple set out and ran towards the tomb. Simon Peter went into the tomb. He saw the linen wrappings lying there, and the cloth that had been on Jesus' head not lying with the linen wrappings but rolled up in a place by itself. Then the other disciple also went in. Then the disciples returned to their homes.

But Mary stood weeping outside the tomb. As she wept, she bent over to look into the tomb; and she saw two angels in white, sitting where the body of Jesus had been lying, one at the head and the other at the feet. They said to her, 'Woman, why are you

287

weeping?' She said to them, 'They have taken away my Lord, and I do not know where they have laid him.' When she had said this, she turned round and saw Jesus standing there. Jesus said to her, 'Woman, why are you weeping? For whom are you looking?' Supposing him to be the gardener, she said to him, 'Sir, if you have carried him away, tell me where you have laid him, and I will take him away.' Jesus said to her, 'Mary!' She turned and said to him in Hebrew, 'Rabbouni!' (which means Teacher). Jesus said to her, 'Do not hold on to me, because I have not yet ascended to the Father. But go to my brothers and say to them, "I am ascending to my Father and your Father, to my God and your God." ' Mary Magdalene went and announced to the disciples, 'I have seen the Lord'.

(John 20.1-18, edited)

THE SCENE

A Letter from Salome to her husband

From Shlomit, faithful wife, to my beloved husband Yitzchak, and to El'azar and all the supporters of our Rabbi Yeshua in Efrayim.

I have so much news to write to you! You won't believe it!

(She writes about the problem of buying spices for Yeshua's body the evening before).

Miryam of Magdala woke us up really early, all four of us who had been out with her the night before. After washing our hands, we wrapped ourselves in our cloaks and went out. There was just the faintest hint of pale sky in the east. We walked down the Mount of Olives, and past the Roman fortress, ignoring the wolf whistles from the soldiers guarding the main gate of the Antonia. We skirted the city wall till we came to the spot where our rabbi had died. As we got closer, we realised that the stone blocking the grave entrance would still be in place. We didn't know if the combined effort of the four of us would be enough to shift it. Perhaps a stranger might help us. We did not want any of the Twelve to get involved - they had almost been arrested two days ago. But when we got there, there wasn't one grave that was shut! We knew it wasn't a popular place because of where it was. It gave me the cold shivers to be right at the spot where our rabbi had suffered that cursed death. But Miryam of Magdala strode straight up to one of the black square openings, and then shrieked! We ran up to her and stood rooted to the spot. In the early morning light we could just see a young man dressed in a white tunic sitting on the body slab on the right-hand side *inside* the grave. We were about to turn tail and flee when he announced, clear as clear,

"'Don't be shocked. You're looking for Yeshua Ish-Natzaret, the crucified one. He has been raised; he isn't here. Look, here is the place they put him."

We were speechless. We didn't know whether to run or stay.

"Go and tell his trainees, and go and tell Shim'on Kefa, that he is going ahead of you.. He's going to the Galil. You'll see him again, just as he said."

Our nerve broke and we ran out of there as if our lives depended on it. When we got half way along the city wall, Miryam of Magdala stopped.

"That man - whoever he was - told us to tell Shim'on Kefa."

"But we don't know where he is," wailed Yochana.

"I have an idea," she replied. *"You go back and tell the rest of the brothers. I'm going into the city. I think I know where he might be."*

Note: In order to write an account of Jesus' resurrection, I put it in the form of a letter from Salome to her husband. Salome was present at both the cross and the empty tomb. But why write? I imagined that Lazarus, or Elaz'ar, thought he might be next on the chief priests' list, so he walked to the town where Jesus sought refuge after he raised Lazarus from the dead (John 11.54). Salome's husband accompanied him because walking alone was dangerous.

COMMENT

1 What are we told?
We have five accounts of Jesus' resurrection.

Paul
One of the earliest accounts is from Paul in 1 Corinthians 15.4-6, c. 56 CE.

- Jesus was raised on the third day
- Seen by Kephas, i.e. Shim'on Kefa or Simon Peter
- Seen by the twelve
- Seen by over five hundred of the brothers at the same time, etc.

Mark 16
The earliest gospel account. In my opinion, written at the same time as Paul's letters:

- Three women go to the tomb at dawn with spices
- They see a young man dressed in white inside the tomb
- He tells them that Jesus has been raised and will go ahead to Galilee

- He tells them to tell the disciples and Peter.
- The women flee.

The gospel ends with 'for they were afraid'; or in Greek 'ephobontou gar'. No Greek books or even paragraph ended with that simple participle. It must have been Mark's equivalent to a series of dots .... i.e. 'to be continued'.

Luke 24

In my opinion Luke collected the material for his gospel in Jerusalem while Paul was in prison around 60 CE. He later included large parts of Mark's gospel.

- More than five women came to the tomb with spices.
- The tomb is empty
- Two men in dazzling clothes tell them that Jesus foretold his death and his rising again
- The women tell the eleven and the rest.
- Jesus appears to Simon (24.34)
- He appears to Cleopas and his companion on the road to Emmaus. (24.13-35)
- He appears to the eleven in the late evening at Bethany (presumably).

John 20

John's gospel was written some time in the first century, in my opinion by a Jerusalem disciple called John.

- Mary Magdalene finds the empty tomb
- She tells Peter and the other disciple
- Peter and the other disciple run to the tomb and are puzzled.
- Mary encounters the risen Jesus.
- She tells the disciples, "I have seen the Lord."
- Jesus appears to the eleven (without Thomas) in the evening.

Matthew 28

In my opinion Matthew is the latest and most 'churchy' of the gospels. He sets the traditions out in an orderly fashion, but he also editorialises. I doubt his unsupported testimony.

- Jewish soldiers guard the tomb.
- Two women go to the tomb at dawn.
- There is an earthquake.
- An angel looking like lightning and with clothes white as snow comes down from Heaven, rolls the stone away and sits on it.
- The guards become like dead men.
- The angel tells the women that Jesus is raised and will go ahead to Galilee.
- Jesus meets them and says the disciples will see him in Galilee.
- The eleven go to Galilee and see Jesus there.

2 The big question

It is clear that Mark and Luke tell essentially the same story. All agree that the first witnesses were women. Mary from Magdala mentioned in all the accounts.

Both Paul and Luke say that the first male disciple to meet Jesus was Simon Peter.

But how can we reconcile Mark's account with three women and John's, where Mary of Magdala is at the tomb on her own?

Specifically, where was Peter?

3 Where was Peter?

It is strange that the young man in Mark 16.7 tells the women to "tell his disciples and Peter". Almost as if they were in separate places. How could that be?

We last met Peter when he was in the courtyard of the high priest's palace, swearing an oath that he had never met Jesus. According to John's gospel this was in the courtyard of the former high priest Annas, straight after Jesus' arrest. How did he get in? Because the unnamed disciple was known to the high priest and vouched for Peter and brought him inside. So he was there when Peter voiced his panicky denial and *'broke down and wept'* (Mark 14.72). A reasonable guess is that the unnamed disciple took charge of Peter and brought him to his own home within the city. I imagine he stayed there the whole of the next day and night, too grief-stricken and ashamed to brave the city streets and find his way to the other disciples who were cowering in Bethany.

Early on the first day of the week, Mary Magdalene realised that the young man/angel at the tomb wanted them to find Peter, and so she went to the house of the unnamed disciple, where she found not only Peter but Jesus' mother. Peter and the unnamed disciple ran to the tomb, then returned leaving Mary weeping there. There Jesus found her.

REFLECTION

1 Evidence

It is the common experience of humankind that people who have died do not come back and hold conversations a few days later. Yet the best interpretation of the recorded history says this is just what did happen. There is a well known book 'Who Moved the Stone?' by Frank Morison. He originally intended to write a book disproving the whole Christian story of Easter but ended up supporting it.

A rabbi Pinchas Lapide wrote 'The Resurrection of Jesus' (2002) in which he said that he used to be a Sadducee (not believing in resurrection) in relation to the story but changed to being a Pharisee, i.e. believing that God did do the miracle, in order to extend the covenant with the Jewish People to the whole world. He is not a Christian because he does not think that Jesus was the Messiah.

Geza Vermes was one of the foremost biblical scholars of his time . He was from a Jewish family, became a catholic priest, then renounced Christianity. In his book 'Jesus the Jew' he concludes:

In the end, when every argument has been considered and weighed, the only conclusion acceptable to the historian must be that the opinions of the orthodox, the liberal sympathiser and the critical agnostic - and even perhaps of the disciples themselves - are simply interpretations of the one disconcerting fact: namely that the women who set out to pay their last respects to Jesus found to their consternation, not a body, but an empty tomb.' (p. 41)

2 Experience
I have known at least two people who have seen Jesus, one an elderly lady in my congregation at Hackbridge, who saw him standing by the lady chapel at the time of communion. Others who, while yet not believing, had convincing experience of Jesus which led to their conversion, were Sadhu Sundar Singh, Metropolitan Anthony Bloom and Robert van Der Weyer ('Guru Jesus').

For most people what convinces them is the experience of the Holy Spirit, encountering the light and life of God within them. When Peter and the apostles were arrested by the Sanhedrin for preaching and put on trial, they replied, *"We are witnesses of these things, and so is the Holy Spirit whom God has given to those who obey him."* (Acts 5.32)

3 Resurrection and the Spirit
The worldwide church follows Luke's account in Acts and celebrates the coming of the Holy Spirit at Pentecost, fifty

days after Easter. Luke also records several 'little Pentecosts' as the Spirit provided special experiences at key moments of the expansion of the Way, see Acts 4.31, 8.17, 10.44, 19.6.

John, however, ties the coming of the Spirit closely to the story of the first Easter Day.

When it was evening on that day, the first day of the week, and the doors of the house where the disciples had met were locked for fear of the Jews, Jesus came and stood among them and said, 'Peace be with you.' After he said this, he showed them his hands and his side. Then the disciples rejoiced when they saw the Lord. Jesus said to them again, 'Peace be with you. As the Father has sent me, so I send you.' When he had said this, he breathed on them and said to them, 'Receive the Holy Spirit. If you forgive the sins of any, they are forgiven them; if you retain the sins of any, they are retained.'

(John 20.19-23)

To me it makes sense to link the Spirit to the Resurrection. The surprising thing about Jesus' resurrection is not the physical miracle, but the chronological one. It came at the wrong time. People expected the resurrection to happen at the end of this present age, But Jesus' resurrection came in the middle of it. What it did, in principle, was to bring heaven down to earth. The first sign of this was the breathing of the Holy Spirit into Jesus' disciples, in line with the prophecy of Ezekiel, *'I will put my spirit within you, and you shall live.'* (Ezekiel 37.14).

This is what Jesus did. He breathed the Spirit into his disciples. The statement about forgiving and retaining sins probably means giving them the authority to lead the new community of Israel, created through Jesus' obedient death on the cross.

SUGGESTION

A simple way to call on the Holy Spirit is to use the following prayer. (It is a shortened version of a Latin prayer for mass at Pentecost).

'Holy Spirit, come to us, kindle in us the fire of your love.'

The music from the Taizé community can be found easily on YouTube.

Mervyn Stockwood, the Anglican bishop of Southwark, went to an international peace conference in Moscow in the 1970's, when Christianity was still very much persecuted there. While he was there he needed a haircut and went to one of their enormous hair cutting salons with rows of chairs and barbers. While cutting his hair, the barber noticed the bishop's ring. He dropped to his knees, kissed the ring, stood up and shouted to the whole establishment, *"Christ is risen! Christ is risen!"*

The actual words, repeated constantly on Easter Day in the Orthodox Church, are, *'Christ is risen! He is risen indeed!'*

A great way to celebrate Easter is to use this ancient Christian response many times during the day: at the peace in church worship, as a grace before meals, on going to bed and on waking up.

Christ is risen!
He is risen indeed!

REV ANDY'S

OTHER BOOKS

Desert nomads
Ancient Egyptian wallpainting

BIBLE IN BRIEF

An easy way to explore the Bible in just six months

This book is for you if

- you are looking for an understandable way into the Bible;
- you want a clear structure arranged into six monthly topics;
- you want to choose for yourself what to read and when to read;
- you want questions to focus your responses to the readings;
- you would like to create your own Bible commentary in the book or online;
- you are curious about what other cultures of the time were saying;
- you like maps and illustrations and timelines;
- you want to end up seriously informed.

"This book does what few others do - it offers a very helpful guide for those looking for a brief overview of the Bible and its story."
Rt Revd Graham Tomlin, Bishop of Kensington

MONTH 1 WEEK 1

BEGINNINGS

Day 1 Genesis 1 + 2.1-3 The beginning of the world
Is the universe 'good'?
"Made in God's image" - what does this mean?

Day 2 Genesis 2.4-end Beginnings - another account
What do men and women need for life to be good?

Day 3 Genesis 3 Our fall from grace
What attitudes do we have that spoil life?

Day 4 Genesis 4 The first murder
What are the causes and consequences of violence?

Day 5 Genesis 6.9 - 7.end The story of the flood
Note: there were several stories of the flood in the ancient Middle East, reflecting some actual event.
How important is it that a remnant survive a catastrophe?

Day 6 Genesis 8 The end of the flood
Noah's first act on leaving the ark was to worship. Why?

Day 7 Genesis 11.1-9 Humanity disunited
Note: Babel is another name for Babylon, the empire that conquered Judah in 587 BC.
"Pride goes before a fall." Does it?

THE OTHER SIDE
STORIES FROM BABYLON

THE GILGAMESH EPIC OF THE FLOOD

*The Gilgamesh Epic was composed around 2000 – 1800 BC.
Gilgamesh tries to find a way to avoid death. Finally he meets
one person to have eternal life – Uta-pishti – who obeyed they
instruction of the god Ea and survived the great flood..*

"Destroy your house and build a vessel... despising
possessions, preserve what has life. Thus load in your
vessel the seed of all creatures." Uta-pishti built a vast
wooden cube, sealed with pitch, 120 cubits on each side,
with six decks.

All that I had I now loaded aboard her ... silver ... gold ...
yea, of the species of all living creatures ...
all my family, kindred, beasts, wild and domestic, and all of
the craftsmen I made enter the vessel.

Swift blew the storm...
it passed over the land like a battle ...
Even the gods were afeared at the deluge, took to flight, and
went up to the heaven of Anu and cowered like dogs.

For six days and nights the wind blew,
and the flood and the storm swept the land.
But the seventh day arriving did the rainstorm subside. I
opened a vent... and I looked at the sea,
the tideway lay flat as a rooftop.
The whole of mankind had returned unto clay.

DISCOVERING PSALMS AS PRAYER

This book is for you if

- you sometimes think that prayer is a strange thing to do;
- you often don't know how to get started with prayer;
- you find the Psalms confusing (let alone the whole Bible!);
- you would like to know how to USE the Psalms in your spiritual life;
- you wonder if other churches in the world have something to teach us;
- you are interested in one person's spiritual journey in prayer.

"In Discovering Psalms as Prayer Andy Roland weaves together the wisdom of a faithful, personal pilgrimage with practical guidance for reading the psalms. It will be a gift to those wanting to make that discovery for themselves. We are in his debt."
Rev David Runcorn: Spirituality Workbook:
A Guide for Explorers, Pilgrims and Seekers;
Love Means Love etc.

FROM CHAPTER 1

THE PROBLEM OF PRAYER

The key problem with prayer is that we have a problem with it. As soon as we say to ourselves, *"I think I'll pray now"*, we (or at any rate, I) are/am faced with an immediate sense of reluctance. It's like starting the car and trying to drive it with the handbrake on.... So we need a strategy.

FROM CHAPTER 4

BUS-FRIENDLY MORNING PRAYER

The three psalms which are central to Syrian Orthodox morning prayers are psalms 51, 63 and 113.

Psalm 51 starts:
Have mercy on me, O God, according to your steadfast love; according to your abundant mercy blot out my transgressions.

The natural ending is at verse 17:
The sacrifice acceptable to God is a broken spirit;
a broken and contrite heart, O God, you will not despise.

Psalm 63 starts:
O God, you are my God, I seek you,
my soul thirsts for you,
my flesh faints for you,
as in a dry and weary land where there is no water.

The natural ending is at verse 8:
My soul clings to you;
your right hand upholds me.

Psalm 113 starts and continues with the theme of praise:

Praise the Lord!
Praise, O servants of the Lord,
Praise the name of the Lord.

For the first time in my life I encountered psalms as prayers which made immediate sense to me. These three psalms are a wonderful ladder, leading from confession through trust to praise. I started using them daily, and found that wherever I was spiritually, something in these three psalms would speak directly to my situation. And by using them every day, I quickly got to know them by heart. Within a fortnight I could pray them anywhere without the need of a book.

My homeward journey to England started a fortnight after my visit to Kurisumala. I got an overnight coach from Madurai to Madras, a 12 hour journey, stopping every two or three hours for comfort breaks. I managed to sleep from half past midnight to 5.00. I remember looking out of the slightly leaking window at the grey rainswept countryside when I woke, praying the three psalms by memory and feeling a real connection with God.

THE BOOK OF JOB

FOR PRIVATE READING, GROUP STUDY AND PUBLIC PERFORMANCE + ESSAY 'THE MEANING OF JOB'

This book is for you if

- you want to reflect on the big questions of life - suffering, injustice, faith;
- you find the Old Testament a bit unwieldy and want a straightforward way into one of the most powerful books in the Bible;
- you want a way to read Job in a week;
- you want to have a fascinating evening in a home group;
- you want to put on a public drama event, e.g. on a Sunday evening in church, to which you can invite friends and neighbours

To understand anything about how Job works, we need to hear it as drama, as an exchange of passionate, difficult speeches. Hence the importance of this 'arrangement', which allows us to enter the space of the writer's imagination and the writer's faith as it is tested, pushed and squeezed, almost rejected, revived, articulated in intense protest and equally intense trust.

Rowan Williams

JOB FOR GROUP STUDY

Job

3:³ 'Let the day perish on which I was born,
  and the night that said,
  "A man-child is conceived."
  ¹¹ 'Why did I not die at birth,
  come forth from the womb and expire?
  ¹² Why were there knees to receive me,
  or breasts for me to suck?
  ¹³ Now I would be lying down and quiet;
  I would be asleep; then I would be at rest
  ¹⁴ with kings and counsellors of the earth,
  where slaves are free from their masters.

  ²⁰ 'Why is light given to one in misery,
  and life to the bitter in soul,
  ²¹ who long for death, but it does not come,
  and dig for it more than for hidden treasures.

Eliphaz

4:² 'If one ventures a word with you, will you be offended?
  But who can keep from speaking?
  ³ See, you have instructed many;
  you have strengthened the weak hands.
  ⁴ Your words have supported those who were stumbling,
  and you have made firm the feeble knees.
  ⁵ But now it has come to you, and you are impatient;
  it touches you, and you are dismayed.
  ⁶ Is not your fear of God your confidence,
  and the integrity of your ways your hope?

THE MEANING OF JOB

Job

The first two chapters of the book of Job relates a series of disasters that befall Job - death and destruction caused by human wickedness; devastation of natural disasters, and finally a physical skin disease causing permanent pain and social ostracism. He has in a short space of time experienced all the worst that life can throw at us. The next 39 chapters are an impassioned debate on the meaning of life in these circumstances. But rather than exploring the problem of suffering, I believe they explore the problem of God.

The Problem of Suffering

People did, and do, ask "Why me?' "Why did this happen?" "Why do bad things happen to good people?" These are questions as widespread as the human race, and as old as history. But the writers of the Bible did not address these questions, just as Jesus did not.

At that very time there were some present who told Jesus about the Galileans whose blood Pilate had mingled with their sacrifices. He asked them, "Do you think that because these Galileans suffered in this way they were worse sinners than all other Galileans? No, I tell you; but unless you repent, you will all perish as they did."

(Luke 13:1-5)

The easiest way to explain suffering is that the people deserved it. It is the argument of Job's friends:

⁵ *'Surely the light of the wicked is put out,
and the flame of their fire does not shine...*

(Job 18.5)

A Greek Orthodox priest at prayer in the Church of the Holy Sepulchre

A WEEK OF PRAYER IN JERUSALEM

A TRAVELLER'S TALE

Experiencing Jerusalem in the 'Week of Prayer for Christian Unity' 2017
with over 170 colour photos

This book is for you if

- you ever wonder what it would be like to visit Jerusalem;

- you want too explore the amazing variety of churches in the holiest Christian city, and their message of peace;

- want to look behind the strident headlines and get a feel for ordinary life in Israel and the Palestinian Territories;

- are prepared to be surprised and even shocked;

- you are confused about the rights and wrongs of Israelis and Palestinians. I hope that hate book will make you more confused, but at a deeper level!

'*Through his easy to read travel diary Andrew Roland gives us a colourful collage of ordinary and extraordinary encounters with Jerusalemites, places and events. Aware of conflicts and contrasts, as well as human interconnectedness, he joined the different churches celebrating the Week of Prayer for Christian Unity in the city, from where they all trace their origins.*'

Rev Eliza Zikmane, Lutheran minister, City of London

MONDAY – TO BE A PILGRIM

On the Mount of Olives

I had a 20 minute walk along the ridge, passing the Makassed Islamic Charitable Hospital (250 beds) and the Princess Basma Centre for Disabled Children to reach my first stop, the Chapel of the Ascension. This is a unique piece of Jerusalem, inhabiting a sort of quiet no man's land between Christians, Muslims and latterly Jews. It is at the highest point of the Mount of Olives, 830 metres above sea level, a small octagonal courtyard which you have to pay 5 NIS to enter. The Crusaders built a charming octagonal cloister to mark the spot where Jesus ascended into heaven 40 days after his resurrection. Walls and a roof were added by Armenian Christians in 1835, turning a charming open-air plaza into a small dark chapel. In the centre, in the bare rock, is a small hollow, traditionally the footprint of Jesus as he launched himself upwards and pushed the rock which was trying to follow him back to earth. It usually has no more than couple of people inside. The leaflet says, *"Visitors come here to cherish the last spot of Jesus on earth, read passages from texts and sermons, chant and light up candles."*

The site is owned by the small mosque next door. The guide and caretaker, Mohammed, said that Christians were always welcome to pray there, and that lots came on Ascension Day. His son is a bus driver and works for an Israeli company - a fact which clearly brought him no joy.

Round the corner is one of my favourite places in Jerusalem, the Church of the Pater Noster (Our Father). Since my last visit they have started charging 10 NIS, but it is still worth it. The first church on the site was built by Constantine's mother Helena about 330 and called the Church of the Apostles, or the Church of the Olive Grove. It was destroyed by the Persians in 614. A Crusader church was built in 1152 but destroyed after Salah-ed-Din's capture of Jerusalem in 1187. Princess Aurelia Bossi bought the site in about 1860 and began searching for the cave where traditionally Jesus had taught his disciples. It has been French-owned ever since. She established a Carmelite convent and built the cloisters and church between 1868 and 1878. Between 1910 and 1915 an underground grotto and the Byzantine church were discovered and partly reconstructed.

So the place is a tranquil mix of open-air buildings and gardens, with the walls of courtyard being covered with translations of the Lord's Prayer in over 160 languages and dialects, such as Sardinian, Welsh and Cherokee. For me the centrepiece was the prayer in Aramaic and Hebrew, the actual languages of Jesus.

The lush green gardens are a real oasis. I saw a small tabby cat being determinedly pursued by a three-legged tom - I assume he won. At the side of the church is a beautiful olive grove with a fantastic view over Jerusalem. I was simply sitting and enjoying the peace when sadly I was told to leave. They close the site at lunchtime, 12.00 - 2.00. In Jerusalem you have to schedule your times of peace and quiet.